School Renewal in the Bifurcated Educational System

This book offers compelling arguments for moving toward the school renewal model (rather than the school reform model) based on strong empirical evidence and real-world renewal work in schools. Drawing on national and project data alongside rigorous analysis, it highlights structural and leadership barriers that have hindered reform over the past twenty-five years and offers essential constructs and tools to bridge the divide in the educational system, including the bifurcation theory, the win-win leadership theory, implementation integrity, integrated school leadership, and leadership density. With validated instruments and actionable frameworks, this work equips researchers and practitioners with innovative methods to drive school improvement. Policymakers will also find guidance on creating enabling conditions for sustainable progress, focusing on responsive, capacity-building approaches rooted in the complexities of contemporary education.

JIANPING SHEN is Professor of Educational Leadership at Western Michigan University, where he holds two named professorships: John E. Sandberg Professor of Education and Gwen Frostic Endowed Chair. He is the recipient of the American Educational Research Association Division A's 2025 Excellence in Research Award. Dr. Shen has published more than 120 journal articles and several books.

SCHOOL RENEWAL IN THE BIFURCATED EDUCATIONAL SYSTEM

Jianping Shen
Western Michigan University

CAMBRIDGE
UNIVERSITY PRESS

Shaftesbury Road, Cambridge CB2 8EA, United Kingdom

One Liberty Plaza, 20th Floor, New York, NY 10006, USA

477 Williamstown Road, Port Melbourne, VIC 3207, Australia

314–321, 3rd Floor, Plot 3, Splendor Forum, Jasola District Centre,
New Delhi – 110025, India

Cambridge University Press is part of Cambridge University Press & Assessment,
a department of the University of Cambridge.

We share the University's mission to contribute to society through the pursuit of
education, learning and research at the highest international levels of excellence.

www.cambridge.org
Information on this title: www.cambridge.org/9781009448666
DOI: 10.1017/9781009448635

First published 2026

Cover credit: cnythzl via Getty Images

A catalogue record for this publication is available from the British Library

Library of Congress Cataloging-in-Publication Data
Names: Shen, Jianping author
Title: School renewal in the bifurcated educational system / Jianping Shen,
Western Michigan University.
Description: Cambridge, United Kingdom : Cambridge University Press, 2026. |
Includes bibliographical references and index.
Identifiers: LCCN 2025038621 (print) | LCCN 2025038622 (ebook) |
ISBN 9781009448642 hardback | ISBN 9781009448635 ebook
Subjects: LCSH: School improvement programs – United States | School
management and organization – United States
Classification: LCC LB2822.82 .S448 2026 (print) | LCC LB2822.82 (ebook) |
DDC 371.200973–dc23/eng/20260113
LC record available at https://lccn.loc.gov/2025038621
LC ebook record available at https://lccn.loc.gov/2025038622

ISBN 978-1-009-44864-2 Hardback
ISBN 978-1-009-44866-6 Paperback

To my wife, Yeqing Wang, and our son, Kevin W. Shen

Contents

Figures

Tables

Acknowledgments

I would like to express my deep gratitude to the colleagues and friends who made this book possible. First, I am especially grateful to my advisor, Dr. John I. Goodlad, who planted the seed of "educational renewal" during my doctoral studies at the University of Washington. I am also deeply thankful to Dr. Jiangang Xia and Dr. Xingyuan Gao for their collaborative research on two foundational elements of this book – Dr. Xia on the relationship between principal and teacher leadership and Dr. Gao on the structural nature of the educational system.

In addition, I would like to thank many other colleagues and friends who contributed to the collaborative research, including (in alphabetical order by last name): Dr. Walter Burt, Dr. Van Cooley, Dr. Robert Leneway, Dr. Xin Ma, Dr. Nancy Mansberger, Dr. Dennis McCrumb, Dr. Louann Bierlein Palmer, Dr. Charles Pearson, Dr. Sue Poppink, Dr. Mark Rainey, Dr. Patricia Reeves, Dr. Gary Wegenke, Dr. Elizabeth Whitten, Dr. Huang Wu, and others.

I wish to provide a full acknowledgment to the original source of the following journal articles, reprinted by permission of Informa UK Limited, trading as Taylor & Francis Ltd. (www.tandfonline.com):

Shen, J. (2023). Theory of bifurcated educational system and its implications for school improvement. *International Journal of Leadership in Education*, 26(2), 223–243. www.tandfonline.com/doi/full/10.1080/13603124.2020.1808708

Shen, J., & Ma, X. (2006). Does systemic change work? Curricular and instructional practice in the context of systemic change. *Leadership and Policy in Schools*, 5(3), 231–256. https://doi.org/10.1080/15700760600805832

Shen, J., Ma, X., Gao, X., Palmer, B., Poppink, S., Burt, W., Leneway, R., McCrumb, D., Pearson, C., Rainey, M., Reeves, P., & Wegenke, G. (2018). Developing and validating an instrument measuring school leadership. *Educational Studies*, 45(4), 1–20. https://doi.org/10.1080/03055698.2018.1446338

Shen, J., Ma, X., Mansberger, N., Bierlein Palmer, L., Burt, W., Leneway, R., Reeves, P., Poppink, S., McCrumb, D., Whitten, E., Gao, X., & Wu, H. (2024). Developing and validating an instrument measuring school renewal: Testing the factorial validity and reliability. *International Journal of Leadership in Education, 27*(4), 875–893. https://doi.org/10.1080/13603124.2021.1930187

Shen, J., Ma, X., Mansberger, N., Gao, X., Bierlein Palmer, L., Burt, W., Leneway, R., McCrumb, D., Poppink, S., Reeves, P., & Whitten, E. (2020). Testing the predictive power of an instrument titled "Orientation to School Renewal." *School Effectiveness and School Improvement, 31*(4), 505–528. https://doi.org/10.1080/09243453.2020.1749087

Shen, J., & Xia, J. (2012). The relationship between teachers' and principals' power: Is it a win-win situation or zero-sum game? *International Journal of Leadership in Education, 15*(2), 153–174. https://doi.org/10.1080/13603124.2011.624643

Xia, J., & Shen, J. (2020). The principal-teacher's power relationship revisited: A national study based on the 2011–12 SASS data. *Leadership and Policy in Schools, 19*(3), 477–496. https://doi.org/10.1080/15700763.2019.1586962

I also wish to provide a full acknowledgment to Sage Publications as the original source of the following journal article and for the permission to reuse some materials in this book:

Shen, J. Gao, X., & Xia, J. (2017). School as a loosely coupled organization? An empirical examination using national SASS 2003-04 data. *Educational Management, Administration & Leadership, 45*(4), 657–681. Copyright © [2016] The Authors. https://doi.org/10.1177/1741143216628533

CHAPTER 1

What We Have Missed

Reflections on the Last Twenty-five Years of School Reform in the US

INTRODUCTION

The purpose of this chapter is to propose a theory to explain why educational reforms fail again and again and to advocate for a new approach to improving schools and student achievement in the US context. The chapter integrates four related sets of empirical studies. After describing the phenomenon of repeated failures of educational reforms and the intractability of school improvement, the first set of empirical studies is introduced to argue that the assumption of a "loosely coupled" system (thus, the approach to school improvement is to tighten the educational system via standards and accountability assessments) is untenable; rather, the educational system is bifurcated, with the state-district-school as one plate and the classroom as the other, resulting in a fault line between the state-district-school and the classroom and the failure of bridging the two tectonic plates. The second set of empirical studies illustrates that the relationship between the principal and teachers is characterized by the "win-win situation," rather than the "zero-sum game." Therefore, it is feasible to promote the concept of integrated school leadership to bridge the fault line. The third set of empirical studies finds that the construct and practice of learning-centered, integrated school leadership are positively related to student achievement. The fourth set of empirical studies reveals that the construct and practice of school renewal predict not only the current level but also the growth of student achievement.

Thus, to bridge the fault line via integrated school leadership, a new school improvement approach – with dual foci on the learning-centered, integrated school leadership as the "content" and school renewal as the "process" – is proposed. This chapter is a synthesis of the earlier four related sets of empirical studies, with relevant key results from these empirical studies presented. The four sets of empirical studies are synthesized for the first time to propose the bifurcation theory and to advocate a new school improvement model, with dual foci on both the content of learning-centered, integrated school leadership and the process of school renewal.

THE ISSUE OF THE INTRACTABILITY OF SCHOOL IMPROVEMENT

How to improve our schools has been a perennial question in American education. In his classic piece, "Reform Again, Again and Again," Cuban (1990) lamented that educational reform had failed repeatedly. In explaining why educational change fails, he moved beyond the argument of a lack of rationality and focused on the political and institutional perspectives. Similarly, Sarason's (1990) book, *The Predictable Failure of Educational Change,* also noted the predictability of the failure of educational reform, primarily from the cultural perspective. So why is school improvement so difficult?

A common theme of the classic studies on the failure of educational reform is that educational reforms could not transform the classroom practice. On this topic, Cohen (1990) has written an insightful essay on why educational change fails, called "A Revolution in One Classroom: The Case of Mrs. Oublier." Oublier is a pseudonym based on the French word meaning "to forget." Cohen studied the teaching practice of Mrs. Oublier, who enthusiastically embraced a new math initiative in the 1980s. She felt she was fluent in the new math language and successful using the new curriculum. However, when Cohen observed her classroom, he found that not much had changed. While her teaching did reflect the new math in many ways (e.g., she adopted the curriculum's innovative instructional materials and activities), Mrs. Oublier "forgot" about the new math as far as her teaching practice was concerned, treating the new mathematical topics designed to help students make sense of mathematics as though she were teaching the old math curriculum. According to Cohen, she has revised the content but taught the class "in ways that discourage(d) exploration of students' understanding" (p. 312), a phenomenon of old wine in a new bottle.

Cohen's (1990) case study was a good example of how difficult it is to change a teacher's classroom instructional practices, even when teachers are enthusiastic about a new curriculum initiative. In concluding his article, Cohen identified the essence of the intractability of the school improvement issue as "whether federal, state, and district mandates to alter schooling will get past the classroom door" (p. 3).

One of the most systematic studies that illustrate how difficult it is for educational reform to penetrate through the classroom door was Goodlad and Klein's (1975), *Looking Behind the Classroom Door*. The book was a summary of the data that Goodlad and his research team collected and analyzed while visiting hundreds of classrooms across the country. Goodlad and Klein (1970) first formulated ten reasonable expectations for classroom instruction based on whether the slogans of educational reform were translated into classroom-level practice. For example, one of the expectations was "individualized instruction," but they did not see much of individualized instruction in classrooms. In fact, to their dismay, Goodlad and his team found that none of these so-called reasonable expectations had been translated into classroom practice.

The issue of the intractability of school improvement continued to be revisited after the seminal work by Goodlad, Cuban, and Cohen. For example, Spillane (1999) demonstrated the complexity of changing teachers' instructional practices. O'Day (2002) suggested that teachers are inclined to metaphorically and literally "close" the classroom door "as a coping strategy that potentially allows them to focus, but it also leads to isolation" (p. 301). Shen and Ma (2006), using a nationally representative sample of teachers from the National Center for Education Statistics (NCES) Schools and Staffing Survey, investigated the relationships among the state's curriculum guidelines, schools' curriculum, and classroom teachers' instruction and found that the influence of states and schools stopped at the classroom door. Later, Bryk et al. (2009) noted that teachers tended "to determine their own objectives and enact instruction accordingly, leading to variation within the same school" (pp. 264–265).

Therefore, one of the reasons that we "reform again, again, and again" – to use the title of Cuban's (1990) article – is that educational reform agendas have not been translated into classroom practice. This begs the question: Why is it so hard to translate educational reform agendas into classroom practice? Why has our field not prioritized bridging the fault line in the bifurcated educational system?

THE THEORY OF LOOSE COUPLING

Weick's (1976) loose coupling theory has been used to explain the intractability of school improvement. Weick's seminal paper, "Educational Organizations as Loosely Coupled Systems," defined "loose coupling" as events that are attached to each other to a certain extent, yet each retains its discrete identity. Over the years, several researchers have studied the application of loose coupling in education, notably Hautala et al.'s (2018) recent integrative review of the literature. As a result, a general mental model that educational organizations are loosely coupled has emerged and essentially become the consensus model.

There have been a variety of reactions to the loose coupling theory applied to educational systems. One school of thought regards loose coupling as a problem to be solved and is interested in employing approaches to tightening the loose coupling (e.g., Fusarelli, 2002; Lutz, 1982; Morley & Rassool, 2000; Smith & O'Day, 1990). The systemic change movement is an example of this approach. Smith and O'Day (1990), for example, regarded the "fragmented, complex, multilayered educational policy system in which they (schools) are embedded" as a "fundamental barrier to developing and sustaining successful schools in the USA" (p. 237). They argued that efforts must be made at the state level in order to target the whole system through an alignment of the intended changes on standards, curriculum, and student tests. By targeting the whole system, the reform efforts could be more consistent and effective. The fundamental assumptions of the systemic change movement are that (a) only systemic reform can tighten the school system and (b) these reform efforts will indeed penetrate all the way down to the classroom level.

Generally speaking, educational reform policies at the federal and state levels in the last twenty-five years have gone down this path of tightening the loosely coupled system. Clinton's Improving America's Schools Act of 1994 established curriculum standards for mathematics and English language arts (ELA), among others. Bush's No Child Left Behind Act of 2002 required, based on curriculum standards, statewide testing and accountability measures for schools, principals, and teachers. Obama's Every Student Succeeds Act of 2015 continued the accountability measures. The strategy in the earlier reauthorizations of the Elementary and Secondary School Act and ensuing state policies was first to develop, promulgate, and implement curriculum standards. Once the curriculum standards were in place, statewide testing of student achievement became possible. With the data from statewide testing, policies were proposed and implemented to hold schools, teachers, principals, and other educators accountable. All of these policy efforts have aimed at tightening the loosely coupled system. As Mason (2001) summarized, the core logic of systemic change is to align a system of standards and instructional guidance at all levels of the educational system, and the alignment is reinforced by accountability measures based on mandatory statewide standardized testing.

Given the seemingly unsuccessful development and implementation of systemic change, researchers have sought to understand how standards-based policy and practice have played out at the district and school levels and have influenced teaching and learning in the classroom (Mason, 2001). Shen and Ma's (2006) study used nationally representative school and teacher samples from the NCES Schools and Staffing Survey to investigate "how the systemic change theory transpired when it was applied to the technical core of teaching and learning" (p. 235). They found that, from the states' guidelines, to the schools' curriculum, to classroom teachers' instruction, systemic change was able to penetrate all the way down to the school level, but again stopped just outside the classroom door.

A BIFURCATED EDUCATIONAL SYSTEM

Empirical studies have continued along this line over the years, testing the relationship between the district and school, and between the school and classroom. As mentioned earlier, Shen and Ma (2006), studying the relationship among the state's curriculum guidelines, schools' curricula, and classroom teachers' instruction, found that the state's curriculum guidelines and schools' curricula were tightly aligned and that the influence of states and schools stopped at the classroom door. Later, Shen, Gao, and Xia (2017) found that the relationship between the school and the classroom in data-informed practices was loose. The summary of the earlier empirical findings, all based on multilevel analyses of nationally representative data, suggests that the educational system is not loosely coupled throughout, as previously thought. Instead, the technical core of the educational system is "bifurcated" – with tight coupling from the state level to the district level and to the school level, and loose coupling from the school level to the classroom level. Borrowing a metaphor from geoscience, it appears that the educational system is composed of two "tectonic plates." One plate includes the state, the district, and the school, and the second plate is the classroom. These two tectonic plates are separated by a "fault line" between them. As documented in previous studies (Bryk et al., 2009; Cohen, 1990; Goodlad & Klein, 1975; O'Day, 2002; Shen & Ma, 2006; Spillane, 1999), "the fault line" is an important reason for the perennial phenomenon of the failure of educational reform because the practices advocated by the reform fail to materialize in the classroom.

The theory of bifurcated systems challenges the conventional wisdom that the educational system is loosely coupled and calls into question the dominant reform agenda for the last twenty-five years, which advocated tightening the system via curriculum standards, accountability tests, and evaluation as the way to improve the K-12 schools. In other words, one of the major issues in educational policy today is that policy initiatives at the federal and state levels are not consistent with the nature of the educational system. As far as the technical core of the schooling – teaching and learning – is concerned, the schooling system is tightly coupled from the state to the school level, but it becomes loosely coupled where classroom-level teaching is concerned. This bifurcation explains the perennial phenomenon of "teachers closing their classroom doors" (Goodlad & Klein, 1975), "reforming again, again, and again" (Cuban, 1990), and the non-event of "revolution in a classroom" (Cohen, 1990).

CLASSROOM DOOR AS A FAULT LINE AND THE ROLE OF PRINCIPALSHIP AND SCHOOL LEADERSHIP

To continue the metaphor of tectonic plates, the theory of bifurcated systems indicates that there is a fault line between the school/principal level, on the one hand, and the classroom level, on the other. Among other implications, the fault line points to the importance of the role of principalship and the concept of integrated school leadership in bridging the fault line.

The Role of Principal Leadership in Bridging the Fault Line between the School and the Classroom

There has been much literature on the role of principals. For example, Portin (2004) and Portin and Shen (2005) summarized principals' roles based on the following observation: Principals remain key individuals as school managers, personnel administrators, problem solvers, boundary spanners, initiators of change, and instructional leaders. While not explicitly stated at the time, embedded in roles such as boundary spanner and instructional leader is the idea that principals must pay attention to bridging the fault line between the school and the classroom. Generally speaking, in both the literature and in practice, this important role of principalship in bridging the two tectonic plates has not been emphasized. Therefore, more attention must be paid to the role principals play in the bifurcated educational system.

The Role of Integrated School Leadership

Given the multiple roles that principals play, they are hailed as "superheroes" (Celio & Havey, 2005). However, principals alone cannot bridge the fault line between the school level and the classroom level. Therefore, we need to promote a strengthening of school leadership through the integration of principal and teacher leadership.

In the literature, there is much evidence about the effect of principal leadership (Leithwood & Louis, 2011; Leithwood et al., 2004; Marzano et al., 2005) and teacher leadership on the success of students and schools (Harris & Muijs, 2003; Reeves, 2008; Wenner & Campbell, 2017; York-Barr & Duke, 2004; Zepeda et al., 2013). However, these theories and models of principal leadership and teacher leadership have been developed on separate and distinct tracks, with studies tending to focus on one and ignoring the other. When principal and teacher leadership are treated separately in either research or practice, it is difficult to estimate the interactional effects of principal leadership and teacher leadership (Leithwood & Jantzi, 1999, 2000). This limitation is not surprising given the classic understanding that the impacts of principal leadership tend to be mediated through teachers, particularly when concerning student achievement (e.g., Hallinger & Heck, 1996a, 1996b, 1998; Leithwood & Jantzi, 2000). To date, very rarely has research focused on the integration of principal leadership and teacher leadership, which can be referred to as "integrated school leadership."

Through comprehensive literature reviews, Hallinger and Heck (1996a, 1996b, 1998, 2011a, 2011b) developed a typology of leadership effectiveness: (a) the direct-effect model (teachers do not interact with principals), (b) the mediated-effect model (teachers passively mediate principals' influence), and (c) the reciprocal-effect model (teachers actively interact with principals). Hallinger and Heck (2010) argued that both the direct and the mediated effects do not fully capture the leadership effects and suggested a reciprocal-effects model to account for the interaction between principal leadership and teacher leadership.

Moreover, given the bifurcated system and the fault line between the school/principal level and the teacher/classroom level, it is more constructive to develop and practice integrated school leadership. Shen and his colleagues conducted an extensive literature review and mapped out the dimensions of integrated school leadership based on comprehensive reviews of the literature. From it, they developed a typology of seven dimensions of learning-centered leadership to understand integrated school leadership, as well as an instrument to measure it (see Figure 1.1 and Table 1.1) (Shen & Burt, 2015; Shen & Cooley, 2012, 2013; Shen et al., 2018).

Figure 1.1 indicates that (a) commitment and passion for school renewal are at the center of learning-centered school leadership and that (b) data-informed decision-making supports the key substantive dimensions of (c) safe and orderly school operation, (d) high, cohesive, and culturally relevant expectations for all students, (e) distributive and empowering leadership, (f) coherent curriculum, and (g) real-time and embedded instructional assessment. Table 1.1 shows the literature base for the seven dimensions of learning-centered school leadership.

These seven dimensions are the integration of principal and teacher leaders because the dimensions encourage principals and teachers to

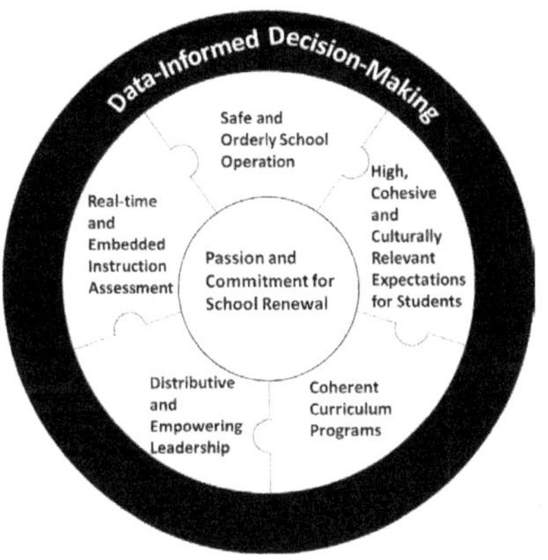

1.1 Seven dimensions of learning-centered school leadership

enter each other's sphere of leadership. Based on the seven-dimension typology of school leadership, Shen et al. (2018) developed and validated an instrument that can be used to measure the collective effort of principals and teachers who exercise their own unique leadership to generate integrated school leadership. It is an instrument called "Learning-Centered School Leadership," which has the earlier seven dimensions or subscales (Figure 1.1 and Table 1.1). Their empirical research indicates that the instrument has sound psychometric properties, including using the subscales and the whole scale to predict school-level student achievement as measured by the state's standardized accountability tests (Shen et al., 2018). In other words, schools that have higher ratings on these dimensions tend to have higher school-level student achievement.

The seven learning-centered leadership dimensions illustrated earlier are examples of integrated school leadership, a combination of both principal and teacher leadership (Shen et al., 2018). They illustrated an image of distributive leadership, but with a content focus, that is, emphasizing those dimensions of work associated with student achievement. They also represented what Cohen (2011) discussed as "capacity" to address the issues associated with the fragmented education system. The construct of integrated school leadership includes the elements of, for example, principal's instructional leadership (R. D. Goddard et al., 2015; Y. L. Goddard et al., 2019) and teacher leadership (Sebastian et al., 2016, 2017; Shen, Wu, Reeves, Zheng,

Table 1.1 *Seven dimensions of learning-centered school leadership and empirical evidence*

Dimensions	Balanced leadership*	Elements in other research
A. Passion and commitment for school renewal	• Affirmation • Change agent • Optimizer • Flexibility • Intellectual stimulation	• Self-efficacy (Smith et al., 2006; Whitt et al., 2015), self-confidence, responsibility, and perseverance; rituals, ceremonies, and other symbolic actions (Cotton, 2003) • Influencing internal school process, such as school policies and norms, teaching practices, and school goals (Crum & Sherman, 2008; Hallinger & Heck, 1996a, 1996b) • The integration of transformational and shared instructional leadership (Marks & Printy, 2003) • Visibility (Witziers et al., 2003) • Purposes and goals (Leithwood & Jantzi, 1999), setting directions (Day et al., 2016; Johnson, 2013; Shatzer et al., 2013; Supovitz et al., 2010; Tan, 2016) • Encouraging teachers to take risks and try new teaching methods (Sebring & Bryk, 2000) • Idealized attributes, behaviors, and inspiration motivation (Allen et al., 2015; Shatzer et al., 2013)
B. Safe and orderly school operation	• Order • Communication • Discipline	• Safe and orderly school environment; positive and supportive school climate; communication and interaction; interpersonal support (Cotton, 2003) • Governance (Heck, 1992; Heck & Marcoulides, 1993); unified governance (Johnson, 2013)

Table 1.1 (*cont.*)

Dimensions	Balanced leadership	Elements in other research
		• Planning, structure, and organization (Leithwood & Jantzi, 1999); redesigning organizations (Day et al., 2016)
		• Minimize classroom disruptions (Sebring & Bryk, 2000)
		• Developing policy with a focus on student learning (Johnson, 2013)
C. High, cohesive, and culturally relevant expectations for all students	• Culture • Focus • Outreach • Ideals/beliefs	• Goals focused on high levels of student learning; high expectations of students; and community outreach (Cotton, 2003)
		• Climate (Heck, 1992; O'Donnell & White, 2005)
		• Leadership of parents is positively associated with student achievement (Pounder, 1995)
		• School mission, teacher expectation, and school culture (Hallinger & Heck, 1996a, 1996b)
		• Defining and communicating mission; achievement orientation (O'Donnell & White, 2005; Witziers, et al., 2003)
		• Culture (Leithwood & Jantzi, 1999; Schrum & Levin, 2013); teacher collaboration culture (Day et al., 2016)
		• Collective efficacy (Goddard, 2001; R. D. Goddard et al., 2004; Manthey, 2006)
		• Collective responsibility (Lee & Smith, 1996)
		• Culturally relevant pedagogy (Boykin & Cummingham, 2001; Dill & Boykin, 2000; Ladson-Billings, 1994, 1995a, 1995b, 1998)

Table 1.1 (*cont.*)

Dimensions	Balanced leadership	Elements in other research
D. Coherent curricular programs	• Curriculum, instruction, and assessment • Knowledge of curriculum, instruction, and assessment	• Instructional organization (Hallinger & Heck, 1996a, 1996b; Heck, 1992; Heck & Marcoulides, 1993) • Integration of transformational and shared instructional leadership (Marks & Printy, 2003; Dutta & Sahney, 2016) • Supervising, coordinating, managing, and evaluating the curriculum (Witziers et al., 2003) • Instructional program coherence (Newmann et al., 2001) • Instructional leadership (Shatzer et al., 2013; Tan, 2016; Whitt et al., 2015)
E. Distributive and empowering leadership	• Input • Resources • Visibility • Contingent reward • Relationship	• Shared leadership/staff empowerment; visibility and accessibility; teacher autonomy; support for risk taking; professional opportunities and resources (Cotton, 2003) • Cultivating teacher leadership for school improvement; shared instructional leadership (Marks & Printy, 2003) • Promoting school improvement and professional development (Witziers et al., 2003) • Developing people (Day et al., 2016; Hallinger, 2011b; Johnson, 2013; Tan, 2016) • Teacher empowerment (Marks & Louis, 1997; Sweetland & Hoy, 2000) • Distribution of leadership (Day et al., 2016; Schrum & Levin, 2013; Tan, 2016); collaborative leadership (Hallinger & Heck, 2010; Heck & Hallinger, 2010)

Table 1.1 (*cont.*)

Dimensions	Balanced leadership	Elements in other research
		• Individual consideration (Allen et al., 2015)
		• Professional community (Louis et al., 1996; Marks & Louis, 1997; Spillane, Halverson, & Diamond, 2001)
		• Social trust (Sebring & Bryk, 2000); trust and collaboration (Supovitz et al., 2010)
		• Engaging community and connecting with district leadership (Johnson, 2013)
F. Real-time and embedded instructional assessment	• Curriculum, instruction, and assessment • Knowledge of curriculum, instruction, and assessment	• Instructional leadership; classroom observation and feedback (Cotton, 2003); observation and performance management (Day et al., 2016) • Instructional organization (Hallinger & Heck, 1996a, 1996b; Heck, 1992; Heck & Marcoulides, 1993) • Transformational and shared instructional leadership (Marks & Printy, 2003; Dutta & Sahney, 2016) • Monitoring student progress (Witziers et al., 2003) • Instructional program coherence (Newmann, et al., 2001) • Active support of instruction (Supovitz et al., 2010)
G. Data-informed decision-making	• Monitor/ Evaluate • Situational awareness	• Opportunity to learn; learning time; and teacher practice (Hallinger & Heck, 1996) • Supervising and evaluating the curriculum (Witziers et al., 2003)

Table 1.1 (*cont.*)

Dimensions	Balanced leadership	Elements in other research
		• Information collection (Celio & Havey, 2005; Leithwood & Jantzi, 1999; Shen & Cooley, 2008; Shen, Cooley, Ma et al., 2012; Shen et al., 2010, 2016a, 2016b) • Organizational learning (Marks et al., 2000) • Use of data (Anderson et al., 2010; Day et al., 2016; Johnson, 2013)

* Elements from Marzano et al. (2005)

Ryan, & Anderson, 2020). The seven dimensions illustrated earlier are just examples of integrated school leadership. More indicators of integrated school leadership should be developed based on practice and research.

Integrated Leadership as a Zero-Sum Game or a Win-Win Situation?

There are deeply rooted doubts about whether it is ever possible to bridge the fault line by integrating principal and teacher leadership. This is because, in the general leadership arena, there is a philosophical debate on whether leadership is zero-sum or win-win. On the one hand, the zero-sum theory posits that the amount of leadership is finite, and the increase of leadership on the part of one player will necessarily reduce leadership on the other player(s). On the other hand, win-win theory postulates that the amount of leadership is expandable, and the leadership pie can grow. The idea of integrated school leadership, which increases the leadership of both the principal and teachers, would be opposed by those who believe in the zero-sum theory. However, empirical research suggests that the power relationship could indeed be a win-win. Shen and his colleague (Shen & Xia, 2012; Xia & Shen, 2020) used the nationally representative data from the NCES Schools and Staff Survey to study the power relationship between the principal and teachers in seven decision-making areas: "set performance standards," "establish curriculum," "determine content of professional development," "evaluate teachers," "hire new full-time teachers," "set discipline policy," and "decide how to spend school budget." Their multilevel modeling indicated that the power relationship between the principal and their teachers was characterized by win-win theory in all decision-making areas, except for the area of "evaluating teachers." This empirical finding supports the idea of integrated school leadership. Integrated school leadership is not a utopian ideal. Rather, it is a practical approach to bridging the fault line between the two bifurcated tectonic plates of the educational system and, ultimately, improving our schools.

MOVING TOWARD SCHOOL RENEWAL: A NEW APPROACH TO SCHOOL IMPROVEMENT

A second principle for school improvement in the bifurcated educational context is the school renewal process, which emphasizes implementation *integrity* by placing less emphasis on the accuracy and completeness of applying a program model and more on the internal conditions and external pressures of a given context. This is counter to conventional lines of research and practice that focus on implementation *fidelity*, which emphasizes the extent to which a project follows a prescribed model (Bond et al., 2000). Proponents of implementation fidelity assert that if we "faithfully" carry out the innovations, we will see results. However, given (a) the bifurcated educational system (i.e., the loose coupling between the school level and the classroom level) and (b) the unique ecology of the implementation sites, to "faithfully" carry out prescribed educational innovations becomes a fantasy that has repeatedly resulted in the failure of educational reform.

Scholars (e.g., Goodlad, 1975a, 1975b; Shen, 1999; Shen & Burt, 2015; Soder, 1999) have been advocating for a model of school renewal to initiate and sustain educational change. There has been sustained research and practice on this topic, with contrasts between "school reform" and "school renewal" developed. For example, Goodlad (1975a, 1975b) distinguished the research, development, dissemination, and evaluation

Table 1.2 *School reform model versus school renewal model*

The "reform" model	The "renewal" model
Shifting focus	Focus on students and their achievement
Driven by the reform agenda	Continuous school improvement
Externally driven	Balance between the internal and external influences
The research, development, dissemination, and evaluation (RDDE) model	The dialogue, decision, action, and evaluation (DDAE) model
Implementation fidelity	Implementation integrity
Implementers as passive receivers	Implementers as active developers
External accountability	Internal responsibility and professionalism

(RDDE) process (associated with school reform) and the dialogue, decision, action, and evaluation (DDAE) process (associated with school renewal); Soder (1999) observed that "you can tell people what to do [reform], or you can let people determine their purposes and ways to achieve them [renewal]" (p. 568). The differences between "reform" and "renewal" could be summarized in Table 1.2.

In most studies on program effects, fidelity was measured as a moderator to explain the variation of the program effects across different sites. Carroll et al. (2007) developed a two-facet framework for implementation fidelity: adherence and moderators. Adherence is the bottom-line indicator of implementation fidelity, which includes four elements: content, coverage, frequency, and duration. The following factors may also influence the degree of fidelity: intervention complexity, facilitation strategies, quality of delivery, and participant responsiveness.

However, Bryk (2016) has indicated that in the social sciences, improvement programs are often designed with high complexity, which involves multiple roles, processes, and tools, as well as interactions among people, and change agents in these improvement programs face a wide range of factors in their organization and local context. In many situations, the program effects are often moderated by these local contextual conditions. Therefore, when designing an improvement program, we must consider what we care about: to know the true effect of our program or to improve a situation using this program. If we emphasize the first purpose, we may care only about the nature of the program itself, while in the latter, we must focus on "the implementation demands that the intervention places on local contexts and organizational structures" (Bryk, 2016, para. 4). Under the first purpose or in a situation Bryk (2016) called "Simple-Simple," where the programs are well defined by explicit sequences of steps and require little change in broad organizational process, implementation with fidelity is the right concept to apply. However, in complex situations, "successful implementation requires learning how to get this intervention to work reliably in the hands of many different professionals working in varied organizational contexts; it is a problem of local adaptive integration" (Bryk, 2016, para. 9). Thus, in those circumstances, it is more sensible to adopt the idea of implementation integrity.

Implementation integrity puts less emphasis on the accuracy and completeness of applying the program model and focuses instead on the given internal conditions and external pressures, that is, what are the most appropriate things to do? That is why the renewal model emphasizes the creative tension between the external and internal influences, a non-linear and vaguely goal-oriented path, implementers as active developers, and the process of DDAE (Shen & Burt, 2015). Even though some researchers argued that the adaption of implementation to different sites may comprise the program's efficacy, the rigid adherence to program procedures is counterproductive to the renewal process (Dane & Schneider, 1998). Moreover, Shen, Yang, Cao, and Warfield (2008) suggested that the adaptations promote program fidelity rather than competing with it. Thus, in education settings, the idea of implementation integrity is more reasonable and feasible given the complex local contexts (LeMahieu, 2011). Finally, implementation integrity empowers schools, principals, teachers, and others to reconceptualize with critical thinking and be creative in developing renewal activities in their unique settings.

One of the issues in improving classrooms is the personal, interpersonal, and organizational capacity that exists within the system (Mitchell & Sackney, 2011). Given the context of the bifurcation theory, the issue of the capacity at the school level, and particularly at the classroom level, becomes even more prominent. The constructs of bifurcation theory, integrated leadership, and school renewal have three implications for policy, practice, and research. First, these constructs provide a perspective that is different from the externally driven reform model, focuses more on the internal responsiveness, and blurs the lines of teacher leadership and principalship to align and increase the capacity at various levels. Second, these constructs also point to those practices that are consistent with school improvement in the context of the bifurcation theory, integrated leadership and school renewal, such as engaging in (a) working in learning communities according to Mitchell and Sackney's (2011) framework (e.g., "the construction of knowledge" in personal capacity, "building the team" in interpersonal capacity, and "leadership for learning" in "organizational capacity"), (b) practicing along the dimensions measured in the instrument titled "Orientation to School Renewal" (Shen et al., 2020), and (c) going outside the school walls to create networked improvement communities (Bryk et al., 2010; Chapman, 2008; Chapman & Muijs, 2014; Wohlstetter et al., 2003). Third, more research is needed to promote the practices of integrated leadership and school renewal in the context of the bifurcation theory. Developing and validating practices for integrated leadership and school renewal to enhance the capacity at various levels should continue to be at the core of the school improvement efforts.

MOVING INTO THE FUTURE: PROMISING EVIDENCE

Two groups of promising evidence start to emerge when employing "school renewal" as an approach for school improvement in the context of the bifurcated educational system. The first group of evidence is the positive correlation between the school's level of renewal activities and student achievement. Working with more than 120 principals and 360 teacher leaders over the years, Shen and his colleagues have gradually distilled the seven dimensions of school renewal (see Table 1.2). They took one more step and developed and validated an instrument called "Orientation to School Renewal" (Shen et al., 2024). Through the validation process, they found that the instrument has good psychometric properties. As to factorial validity, the comparative fit index (CFI) was 0.931, the Tucker-Lewis index (TLI) 0.913, and the standardized root mean square residual (SRMR) 0.037, all indicating good data-model fit.

As to reliability, the internal consistencies (Cronbach's alpha) across the seven factors of school renewal ranged from 0.807 to 0.923 and for the whole instrument 0.974, all above the typical 0.80 cutoff value. Therefore, the mental model of the seven dimensions of school renewal has good factorial validity and reliability, and the seven dimensions of school renewal are supported by the empirical data.

More importantly, Shen and his colleagues went one step further to test the predictive power of the instrument and found that the ratings on the school renewal instrument, both the subscales and the whole scale, are generally able to predict not only the school's current student achievement but also the growth in student achievement on the Michigan Student Test of Educational Progress (M-STEP). In other words, if a school is rated higher in terms of the level of the school renewal efforts as measured by the instrument, the school's student achievement level tends to be higher and grow more. For example, as to the gain in student achievement, a one-unit increase (on the measurement scale of 1–6) in school renewal efforts was associated with 4.23 and 2.74 percentage points higher from the prior to the current year in terms of the gain in proportion of students who reached the proficient and advanced categories in mathematics and ELA, respectively, at the grade level. They also found that the multiple regression models accounted for 65 percent of the variance in gains in the proportion of students who reached the proficient and advanced categories in mathematics at the grade level and between 62 percent and 64 percent of the variance in gains in the proportion of students who reached the proficient and advanced categories in ELA at the grade level. These percentages were highly substantial, indicating great performance of the multiple regression models in accounting for the variance in gains in the proportion of students who reached the proficient and advanced categories in both mathematics and ELA at the grade level (Shen et al., 2020). Therefore, the instrument could be used as a tool to guide and monitor the school renewal process, an effort that is effective given the context of the bifurcated system.

The second group of evidence to support the concept of "school renewal" is the actual school improvement that took place in schools. Through the Learning-Centered Leadership Development Program funded by the School Leadership Program of the US Department of Education, fifty schools were engaged in the school renewal process as described in Table 1.2 to develop, implement, and evaluate school renewal activities. As a result, evidence of positive effects emerged. First, participating schools reported that the school renewal process helped the development of the renewal activities and that the renewal activities were sustained. About one year after the schools completed the project, 73–93 percent of the principals surveyed chose "most of it" or "all of it" regarding whether the renewal activities developed and implemented along the seven dimensions of learning-centered school leadership were sustained (Reeves et al., 2014). One of the reasons for the sustainability is that the renewal activities were developed together by the principal and teachers to address the unique needs of the school. Second, principal leadership has been statistically significantly improved as measured by (a) Vanderbilt Assessment of Leadership in Education (VAL-ED) and (b) Data-informed Decision-Making on High-Impact Strategies (DIDM). Compared to principals in the control group, those in the experimental group improved over a 2.5-year period by 0.52 more on a 5-point scale for VAL-Ed and 0.42 points more on a 4-point scale for DIDM. Both results were statistically significant. Third, the successful school renewal activities and the learning from these cases were documented in eight case studies, with the school as the unit of analysis (Shen, 2015). The summary across these eight case studies suggested that school renewal activities penetrated classroom doors and improved student learning in these high-needs schools by (a) having integrated school leadership to blur the line between principal and teacher leadership, (b) facilitating teachers' investment and engagement in initiating and implementing school renewal activities that have implications for classroom instruction, and (c) improving the overall climate of the school, particularly the expectations for teachers and how to meet these expectations (Poppink, 2015).

SUMMARY

Educational reforms fail again and again. One major reason for the failure is the absence of bridging the fault line between the two tectonic plates in the bifurcated educational system. The dominant educational reform initiatives in the last twenty-five years have focused on the mechanisms for tightening the loosely coupled educational system. This focused attention on curriculum standards, statewide accountability testing, and evaluation of the school and educator was based on the misguided conventional wisdom that the educational system is loosely coupled from the state down through to the classroom. Instead, the educational system is a bifurcated system, with the connected space between the state, district, and school being one tectonic plate, and the classroom another tectonic plate, with a fault line between the two. The theory of bifurcated systems not only explains why educational reforms stop at the classroom door but also raises the key issue of how to bridge the fault line between the two tectonic plates.

In the context of the theory of bifurcated systems, two principles are proposed for school improvement. The first principle is to integrate principal leadership and teacher leadership to develop and practice the construct of integrated school leadership. One model for the school leadership is the seven dimensions of learning-centered leadership. The second principle is the renewal process that emphasizes implementation integrity, versus the reform model that emphasizes fidelity. Reform stops outside the classroom door, while the renewal process penetrates it, helping to transform classroom instructional practices that increase student achievement. The first principle focuses on the content, and the second on the process. The combination of these two principles helps bridge the fault line and improve our schools. The improvement of our schools is reflected in not only enhancing learning for all students but also achieving equity within and between schools for various subgroups of students based on gender, race, language, socioeconomic status, specialized service designations, and others.

The empirical bases of the current article – such as (a) the structural nature of the school system (loosely coupled, tightly coupled, or bifurcated), (b) the nature of the relationship between the principal and teachers in various professional domains (a zero-sum game or win-win situation), (c) the seven dimensions of learning-centered, integrated school leadership, and (d) the seven dimensions of school renewal – have been developed solely in the US context, which is a limitation of the current chapter. Similar studies could be conducted in other countries to investigate, for example, the structural nature of the school system, the nature of the power relationship between the principal and teachers, and leadership constructs and practices based on the findings on the structural nature of the system and the power relationship in the system. The findings from similar studies in other countries could yield insights for school improvement, particularly for how to raise student achievement. A new topic for research – how to improve the relationship between and among various levels of the structure of the educational system to enhance student achievement – appears to emerge.

CHAPTER 2

The Structural Nature of the Educational System

Loosely Coupled or Bifurcated

INTRODUCTION

During the past decades, the issue of loose coupling in the educational system has been one of the most controversial topics in the discourse about educational change. In a school setting, discussions usually refer to the "loose coupling" between school-level administration and classroom-level instruction. Some researchers regarded the "loose coupling" as a natural feature of the educational system and suggested that educational change should take advantage of the "loose coupling" (Goldspink, 2007; Meyer & Rowan, 1978), while other researchers regarded "loose coupling" as a problem to be solved and were interested in the approach to tightening the loose coupling (Fusarelli, 2002; Lutz, 1982; Morley & Rassool, 2000; Smith & O'Day, 1990). In this chapter, we used empirical findings to develop and support a modified theory – the educational system in the US is bifurcated, rather than loosely coupled throughout the system – with an intention to shed some light on the approaches to educational change.

SCHOOLS AS LOOSELY COUPLED ORGANIZATIONS

Weick was one of the researchers who provided the most comprehensive argument for the concept of "loose coupling" (Firestone & Wilson, 1985; Fusarelli, 2002). "Loose coupling," as Weick (1976) proposed, meant that events were attached to each other to some degree; however, each event retained its own identity. Weick (1976) argued that the traditional, bureaucratic way of management only worked well with those tightly coupled organizations, while school systems were in fact very loosely coupled. Meyer and Rowan (1978) contended that educational organizations lacked close internal coordination in both bureaucratic and collegial aspects, especially for instructional activity. They pointed out that "loose coupling" was a result of weak centralized governmental and professional controls.

There have been some modifications to the blanket statement "schools as loosely coupled organizations." For example, Deal and Celotti (1980) observed that administrators could approach their subordinates through informal channels such as acting as "colleagues" or "symbolic leaders" to overcome the looseness of the educational system. Similarly, Firestone and Wilson (1985) reported that through cultural linkages, principals could influence teachers' instruction. They posited that although bureaucratic linkages were necessary to provide restraints and opportunities for teachers, cultural linkages could serve to shape teachers' awareness about "how they think about what they do," including the "individual's definition of the task" and the "individual's commitment to the task" (Firestone & Wilson, 1985, p. 13). They further emphasized the interactions between bureaucratic linkages and cultural linkages, warning that if the two linkages were not matched, there could be counter-productive results.

Ingersoll (1993) also argued that whether a school is loosely coupled depends on the domains of control. He suggested schools could be regarded as "tightly coupled" in certain domains, if researchers "look beyond oversimplified notions of bureaucracy and take into account a range of possible mechanisms of control" (Ingersoll, 1993, p. 105). To illustrate this idea, Ingersoll (1994) examined the power domain of teachers and principals. He found that from the social function of schooling to classroom-level activities, teachers had more and more control. Another follow-up empirical study by Ingersoll (1996) showed that teachers lacked power over sorting and socialization functions in schools, but they reported having autonomy over instruction and curriculum in the classroom. Ingersoll argued that a school was loosely coupled as far as the classroom was concerned but was tightly controlled when it came to the school's sorting and socialization functions.

OBDURACY OF THE "TECHNICAL CORE"

The classroom is the central arena in the school system (Deal & Celotti, 1980). Correspondingly, the technical core is generally considered as the central piece of "loose coupling" (Bryk et al., 2009; Elmore, 2000; Meyer & Rowan, 1978). Elmore (2000) reviewed previous work on loose coupling and offered a definition for "technical core":

> detailed decisions about what should be taught at any given time, how it should be taught, what students should be expected to learn at any given time, how they should be grouped within classrooms for purposes of instruction, what they should be required to do to demonstrate their knowledge, and, perhaps most importantly, how their learning should be evaluated – resides in individual classrooms, not in the organizations that surround them (Elmore, 2000, p. 6).

Many scholars have written about the intractability of the "technical core." Goodlad and Klein (1975) wrote a book entitled *Looking Behind the Classroom Door* and found that teachers continued their practice regardless of the rhetoric of the reforms. Cohen (1990) compared a teacher's actual practice with the new mathematics teaching policy of the California State Department of Education and noticed that even for a teacher with enthusiasm about revolutionizing the classroom, her teaching behaviors seemed unalterable. A study conducted by Spillane (1999) also revealed the complexity of changing teachers' instructional practice. As O'Day (2002, p. 300) postulated, teachers tended to "close" the classroom door simply because teachers' work was "subject to continual interruption as others try to thrust new information upon them," even worse, "much of the information was irrelevant to the improvement of instruction and learning." Bryk et al. (2009, pp. 264–265) noted that if the technical core is not well articulated for all teachers, they are inclined to "determine their own objective and enact instruction accordingly, leading to variation within the same school."

There appears to be more consensus on the intractability of the technical core in the context of a loosely coupled system than on how to deal with the intractability. Both managerialism and professionalism claim to be able to improve the technical core, yet through different techniques. Supporters of managerialism advocate for tightening the system from the top-down, and establishing order and accountability. For example, Spillane et al. (2011) suggested that by redesigning organizational routines, it is possible to regulate the instructional program, set and maintain direction, and transform classroom instruction. Supporters of professionalism, on the contrary, believe that "educational reform's progress depends on teachers' individual and collective capacity" (Stoll et al., 2006, p. 221), therefore, teachers themselves are supposed to be the heroes who remove the intractability of the technical core. They argue that loose coupling is the nature of the educational organization; to reach the technical core, educational improvement needs to be developed from the bottom-up.

A PARADIGMATIC DEBATE ON THE RELATIVE ADVANTAGES AND DISADVANTAGES OF LOOSE COUPLING

In the literature, there has been a consensus that the school system is a loosely coupled system. However, there are widely differing ideas on how to deal with the "looseness" in the context of educational improvement. For example, Orton and Weick (1990) enumerated and reviewed the advantages and disadvantages of loose coupling based on their review of 300 papers. There is essentially a paradigmatic debate on how to take into account the relative advantage and disadvantage of loose coupling. On the one hand, the proponents of the managerialist paradigm argued that loose coupling is a problem and the key to educational improvement is to find mechanisms to tighten the educational system (Morley & Rassool, 2000). Managerialism, according to Goldspink (2007, p. 27), is "an application of business management principles to public institutions." The systemic change in the US reflected the effort to tighten the loosely coupled system by publishing curriculum standards, developing accountability tests, and providing rewards and sanctions based on the results of the accountability test (Fusarelli, 2002; Smith & O'Day, 1990). Those who saw the relative disadvantage of loose coupling tended to advocate a top-down approach with a change model for the bureaucratic realm.

On the other hand, there are also those who believed the educational system was loosely coupled by nature and the key to educational improvement was to find ways to take advantage of the loose coupling. Those who saw the relative advantage of loose coupling tended to advocate a bottom-up approach with a change model for the complex professional system. For example, in his Best Paper of the Year 2007 declared by Educational Management Administration & Leadership, Goldspink (2007) proposed a model of school improvement that worked with, rather than against the loosely coupled system. Typically, those who paid more attention to teachers' professional lives tended to use concepts such as professional learning community for educational improvement in the context of a loosely coupled system (Harris & Jones, 2010; Stoll et al., 2006).

Given the paradigmatic difference between those who advocated for systemic change to tighten the loosely coupled educational system and those who argued for accepting loose coupling while strengthening professionalization, this chapter contributes to the paradigmatic debate on loose coupling by providing empirical evidence on whether loose coupling characterizes the relationship between teacher-level data-informed instruction and school-level data-informed improvement efforts, an area where the proponents of systemic change assume that we might see the strongest effect of tightening the system. In the following sections, we provide a more detailed review of systemic change and data-informed decision-making, both of which were important tools advocated by the US Department of Education in order to push the education reform movement to different levels of the education system.

SYSTEMIC CHANGE AS A STRATEGY TO TRANSCEND THE LOOSELY COUPLED SYSTEM

Although some scholars in the 1970s tended to take "schools as loosely coupled organizations" as the raison d'être of the school system (Meyer & Rowan, 1978), since that time, others, such as those in favor of systemic change, have viewed tightening the loosely coupled education system as a mechanism for educational improvement. Because precise technical requirements for instruction are difficult to define, a high-stakes environment was believed to play an important role in tightening the loosely coupled system (Pajak & Green, 2003). As the federal and state governments have become the leading force in the current education reform process in the US, school systems are facing increasing demands for overall increased performance (Fusarelli, 2002). The core idea of systemic change is an aligned system of standards and instructional guidance at all levels of the educational enterprise, reinforced by accountability measures based on mandatory standardized testing (Mason, 2003).

Pointing out that the past reforms of education were limited by their scope, Smith and O'Day (1990, p. 237) suggested "fragmented, complex, multi-layered educational policy system in which they (schools) are embedded" was a "fundamental barrier to developing and sustaining successful schools in the USA." They argued that the state was the one that could target the whole system, and that through an alignment of intended changes on standards, curriculum, and tests by states and districts, the reform efforts could be more consistent and effective. As is assumed, the systemic change is expected to overcome the looseness of the school system and penetrate all the way to the classroom level.

Given the development of systemic change, researchers sought to understand how standards-based policy and practice played out at the district and school levels and influenced teaching and learning in the classroom (Mason, 2003). In a study conducted by Shen and Ma (2006, p. 235), the authors investigated "how the systemic change theory transpires when it was applied to the technical core of teaching and learning within a loosely coupled system." They found an increasingly attenuating relationship from the states' guidelines to the schools' curriculum and to classroom teachers' instruction. In other words, they found that systemic change was able to penetrate all the way to the school level but stopped just at the classroom door.

OUR STUDIES ON THE NATURE OF THE EDUCATIONAL SYSTEM: THE EMERGENCE OF THE BIFURCATION THEORY

The discussion in this chapter indicates that the literature related to the nature of the educational system and the practice related to educational change are dominated by the loose coupling theory. There are different responses to the loose coupling theory, but the responses tend not to examine the loose coupling theory itself. A few large-scale, empirical studies have been conducted using national datasets to test the assumptions of the loose coupling theory. Findings from these empirical studies modify the loose coupling theory. The school system is not loosely coupled throughout. Instead, the system appears to be tightly coupled from the state to the district and to the school; it is the classroom that is loosely coupled from the rest. We call it the theory of a bifurcated educational system, or bifurcation theory for short, or the theory of two tectonic plates (the state-district-school tectonic plate and the classroom tectonic plate).

Study 1: Does Systemic Change Work? Curricular and Instructional Practice in the Context of Systemic Change

Shen and Ma (2006) conducted a study investigating whether systemic change had effectively penetrated this loosely coupled system to influence the technical core – teaching and learning. The systemic change in the 1990s has been a major focus in educational reform (e.g., Clune, 1993; Cohen, 1995; Fuhrman, 1993a, 1993b; O'Day & Smith, 1993; Smith & O'Day, 1990). The core idea of systemic change is that states establish guidelines, frameworks, and benchmarks for curriculum, aligning them with assessment systems to hold schools accountable. However, the traditional educational system has been characterized as "loosely coupled." Therefore, Shen and Ma (2006) asked, among others, the question "To what extent has systemic change penetrated different levels of the educational system (state, school, teacher)?" Their purpose was to inquire into the extent to which systemic change had influenced curriculum and instruction.

Their study utilized data from the Schools and Staffing Surveys (SASSs) from 1987–1988 and 1999–2000, a national survey that collects data, among others, on teachers' perceptions of educational practices. They examined teachers' perceived influences on six key curricular and instructional activities:

- Establishing curriculum
- Determining the content of in-service professional activities
- Selecting textbooks and instructional materials
- Selecting content, topics, and skills to be taught
- Selecting teaching techniques
- Determining the amount of homework assigned

Recognizing the multilevel nature of the educational system (teachers nested within schools, schools nested within states), they used a multilevel modeling approach for the analysis and included the levels of state, school, and teacher in the analysis to ascertain the possible shift of influence at the state, school, and teacher level given the systemic change with the purpose of overcoming the looseness of the educational system.

The key finding from the analysis is that systemic change had influenced the state and school levels, but not the classroom level. Systemic change had successfully influenced curriculum-related policies at the state and school levels but has not significantly altered teaching practices at the classroom level. The proportions of variance attributable to states and schools decreased between 1987–1988 and 1999–2000, particularly in curriculum-related areas such as textbook selection and content to be taught. This suggests that schools and states had increasingly conformed to standardized curricular frameworks. However, the variation at the teacher level remained high, meaning individual teachers continued to vary greatly in their influence on how the curriculum and instruction were implemented in their classrooms. The study highlighted that classroom instruction remains largely resistant to top-down reforms. Even in disciplines with greater state oversight, such as secondary mathematics, the autonomy of teachers in the classroom remains largely intact.

The findings suggest that under the influence of systemic change, the practice at the state and school levels becomes more standardized. However, the classroom level was intact. The findings seem to suggest that from the state to the school, it was not as loosely coupled as the loose coupling theory postulates. It is the classroom level that is loosely coupled from the rest of the educational system. Thus, the educational system seems to be bifurcated, from the state to the school is one tectonic plate, and the classroom is the other.

Study 2: School as a Loosely Coupled Organization? An Empirical Examination of the Relationship between Data-Informed Decision-Making at the School and Classroom Levels Using SASS 2003–2004

The rise of data-informed decision-making (DIDM) in education has transformed how schools evaluate performance and improve instruction. With the expansion of accountability measures and technological advancements, the use of data in education became more prominent. The No Child Left Behind Act (NCLB) of 2002 reinforced the need for data-driven evaluations, requiring schools to use standardized test results, among others, for accountability and improvement (Mandinach et al., 2006). DIDM has since evolved into a key strategy, influencing decisions at multiple levels, from district planning to classroom instruction (Coburn & Turner, 2012). Research highlights three primary uses of data in schools: informing instruction, developing support plans for struggling students, and setting goals and performance targets (Supovitz & Klein, 2003). While district-level DIDM primarily focuses on program evaluation, school-level DIDM is used more for instructional adjustments (Halverson et al., 2007). Despite its growing importance, challenges remain in determining what types of data to use, how to interpret them effectively, and how to translate insights into actionable classroom practices (Honig & Coburn, 2008; Ingram et al., 2004). As data collection and analysis continue to expand, DIDM plays an increasingly central role in shaping educational strategies and student learning outcomes.

Given the emphasis on DIDM and the assumption that DIDM was a powerful tool in aligning the practice at various levels of the educational system, Shen et al. (2017) tested the loosely coupled theory by examining the relationship between school- and teacher-level DIDM, with the purpose of understanding whether and if so, how, the practice of data-informed improvement efforts at the school level are associated with the practice of data-informed instruction by teachers at the classroom level (i.e., the technical core), in the context of systemic change and accountability, which try to transcend the looseness of the school system. Using a nationally representative dataset from the 2003–2004 School and Staffing Survey (SASS), the authors employed a two-level hierarchical linear model. Their key research question was "To what extent is teachers' DIDM related to school-level DIDM?" Figure 2.1 illustrates the conceptual framework for the study.

In addition to many background variables from the teacher, principal, and school surveys, the following were the key variables used in modeling the relationship between principal- and school-level DIDM and teacher-level DIDM. Three variables were extracted from the teacher survey for teacher-level data-informed practices: the extent to which using students' state or district achievement test scores (a) to group students into different instructional groups by achievement or ability, (b) to assess areas where the teacher needs to strengthen the content knowledge or teaching practice, and (c) to adjust the curriculum in areas where

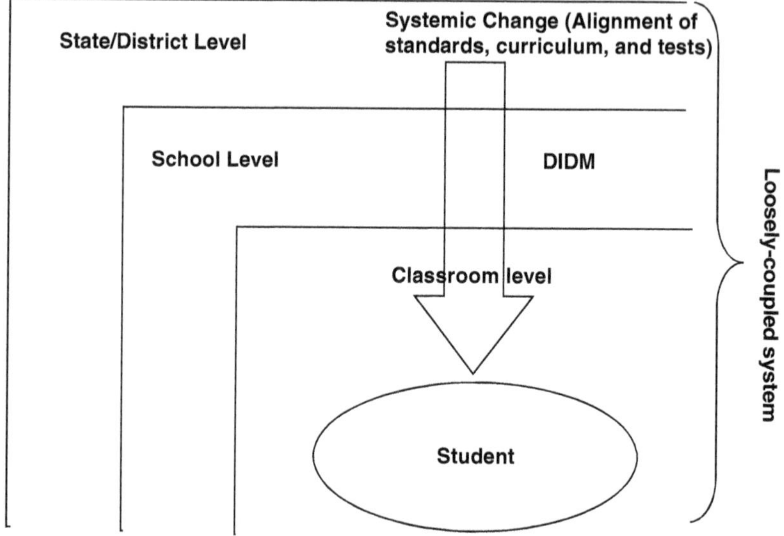

2.1 Conceptual framework

students encountered problems, on a four-point scale ranging from "Not at all" to "To a great extent." Three key variables were extracted from the principal survey for principal-level DIDM: if the principal uses (a) state or national tests, (b) parent or student survey(s), and (c) student portfo-lios to assess the school's progress on the school improvement plan. Five key variables were extracted from the school survey for the school-level DIDM: if using performance reports (covering such things as students' scores on achievement tests or graduation rates) to (a) evaluate the pro-gress of students in this school, (b) determine the next year's instruc-tional focus, (c) realign the curriculum, such as with content standards and/or other indicator criteria, (d) inform parents and the commu-nity of the school's progress, and (e) prompt school-level initiatives for improvement. The DIDM variables from the principal and school surveys covered both what data to use and how to use the data. During modeling, the key variables from principal and school surveys were entered at the second level.

The results indicated that approximately 14.4 percent of the variance in teacher-level DIDM could be attributed to school-level factors. This suggests that while schools exert some influence over teachers' instruc-tional decision-making, much of the process remains independent. The statistical analysis reveals weak associations between school-level DIDM and classroom-level practices. These findings reinforce the theory that the school and the classroom are indeed loosely coupled. The external pressures and administrative strategies have limited impact on the instructional core.

Further analyses using the composite DIDM scores at the school and principal levels and teacher level indicated that the school- and principal-level DIDM had a weak association with teacher-level instructional DIDM as reflected in the small proportion of variances explained and the small effect size for coefficients. Even more detailed analyses revealed that significant associations only existed between teacher-level data-informed instruction and two specific school- and principal-level DIDM strategies: (a) principals' use of state or national tests to assess school progress and (b) schools' use of performance reports to determine the next year's instructional focus; while all other school- and principal-level data-informed efforts were not associated with teacher-level data-informed instruction. The two significant associations were also weak, as indicated by small proportions of variance explained and small effect sizes of the coefficients.

This study provided empirical evidence that schools, particularly at the instructional level, continued to operate as loosely coupled organizations even when DIDM was used as a lever to overcome the looseness in the system. Despite systemic reform efforts, reinforced with accountability measures based on data, aimed at tightening school structures, classroom instruction remained largely autonomous. The findings confirmed that the school and classroom remained loosely coupled in the age of DIDM and challenged the assumption that top-down mandates can effectively drive instructional change.

THE THEORY OF BIFURCATED EDUCATIONAL SYSTEM AND ITS IMPLICATIONS

The issue of loose coupling in the educational system has been a classic and controversial topic in discussions about educational change. Traditionally, researchers have debated whether the education system is inherently loosely coupled or whether efforts should be made to tighten these structures. The two studies (Shen & Ma, 2006; Shen et al., 2017) illustrated earlier provide empirical evidence for the theory of the bifurcated educational system. The educational system is tightly coupled from the state to the school, while the classroom is loosely coupled from the rest of the educational system. This structural divide can be conceptualized, to use a term from geosciences, as two tectonic plates – the state-district-school plate and the classroom plate – where a significant fault line exists between them.

The bifurcation theory is a modification of the traditional loose coupling theory. Instead of viewing the entire educational system as loosely coupled, the bifurcation theory highlights that the primary point of loose coupling occurs between the classroom and the rest of the system. Thus, the focus for school improvement should focus more on the fault line between the classroom and rest of the system. The bifurcation theory has the following implications for school improvement.

First, the bifurcation theory could be used to explain the failure of educational reform initiatives. The externally generated, top-down change initiatives with a focus on implementation fidelity and accountability tend not to work because these initiatives do not take into account the fault line. Change initiatives driven externally tend to rely on administrative mechanisms for implementation. The empirical findings imply that from the state to the district and to the school levels, the administrative mechanisms alone might work. However, administrative mechanisms alone might not be enough to transcend the fault line. Other mechanisms – such as cultural, professional, organizational, etc. – must be considered to transcend the fault line and transform the classroom practices.

Second, the bifurcation theory points to the need to refocus efforts on school improvement. While systemic reforms have, to a great extent, standardized policies at the state, district, and school levels, they have largely failed to transform the classroom, leaving curricular, instructional, and assessment practices at the classroom level loosely coupled from the rest of the system. This persistent disconnect suggests that school improvement efforts must go beyond policy alignment and administrative mandates to engage particularly teachers in the process of change. Strengthening professional learning communities, enhancing teacher agency in decision-making, and fostering meaningful professional and cultural linkages between the principal and teachers are critical strategies for bridging this gap. Rather than relying solely on external mandates, school improvement initiatives should focus on strengthening the instructional core by aligning systemic goals with the realities of classroom teaching while developing teacher capacity and supporting teacher agency in the technical core of curriculum, instruction, and assessment.

Third, the bifurcation theory posits that school is a critical unit for change because school is an organic whole and the fault line occurs within the school. Educational changes could take place at various levels, ranging from teacher certification requirements at a macro-level to an instructional strategy in introducing the concept of fractions at the third-grade level. The bifurcation theory focuses more on the meso-level, that is, the school, because school is not only an organic whole that has all the elements that are necessary and sufficient to transform the classroom, but also a unit where the fault line exists and the actual work to bridge the fault line takes place.

Finally, the bifurcation theory postulates the need to integrate principal and teacher leadership (i.e., integrated school leadership) as an important vehicle to bridge the fault line and transform the classroom practices. Given that the primary disconnect in the educational system exists between the school and the classroom, leadership at the school level – both from the principal and teachers – is essential for fostering coherence and driving instructional change. Principals, as instructional leaders, play a key role in creating an environment where teachers feel supported in using data, engaging in professional learning communities, and aligning their classroom practices with school-wide goals. At the same time, teacher leadership is crucial in developing the school-wide improvement plan, and ensuring that instructional strategies are not merely dictated from above but are informed by the realities of daily teaching and learning and teachers' own sense of professional responsibility. Integrated leadership models that empower teachers to take an active role in decision-making can create stronger linkages between school policies and classroom implementation. By integrating principal and teacher leadership, schools can function as dynamic learning organizations where meaningful changes in curricular, instructional, and assessment practice take place, ultimately improving school and student outcomes.

CHAPTER 3

The Relationship between Principal and Teacher Leadership

A Win-Win Situation or Zero-Sum Game

INTRODUCTION

In the literature of leadership and policy in general, and educational leadership and policy in particular, there are various arguments regarding "Is the amount of power a fixed pie or an expandable pie?" or, to put it in another way, "Is the power relationship between or among actors a zero-sum game or win-win situation?" The metaphor of a fixed power pie assumes the zero-sum game theory – with one party gaining more power, the other party or parties necessarily losing power. The metaphor of an expandable power pie points to the win-win situation theory – with actors gaining power simultaneously. As the next two sections will indicate, there are substantial advocacies for both theories.

FIXED POWER PIE AND ZERO-SUM GAME

"Zero-sum" means a situation "in which a gain for one must result in an equal loss from another or others" (Neufeldt, 1991, p. 1554). The term is widely used in literature related to economics, business, and political science. In this chapter, the term "zero-sum game" is used to denote a situation in which a gain in the principal leadership results in a loss in teacher leadership, or a gain in teacher leadership leads to a loss in the principal leadership. In other words, under the zero-sum game theory, there is a negative correlation between the principal leadership and teacher leadership.

In the literature of educational leadership and policy, the "fixed power pie" or the "zero-sum game" is explicitly discussed or implicitly implied. Owens and Valesky (2007) noticed that when the school is conceptualized as a traditional bureaucracy, which emphasizes the top-down exercise of hierarchical power, the leadership of the principal is generally viewed as being in conflict with that of teachers. Blasé and Kirby's study (2008) confirmed this view. In their conversations with school administrators, they often hear principals complain: "why should I let them deal the cards, after all, we were hired to run the school" (p. 41). These conflicts and complaints reflect the mental model that the amount of leadership is finite and an increase of the amount of leadership for one actor will necessitate a decrease of power for another actor. Thus, the leadership relationship is a zero-sum game. According to Covey, people's scarcity mentality is the primary trait of the zero-sum game: "They see life as having only so much, as though there were only one pie out there. ... The scarcity mentality is the zero-sum paradigm" (Covey, 1989, p. 219).

The zero-sum game theory is ubiquitous in the literature. For example, Owens and Valesky (2007, pp. 317–319) adapted Tannenbaum and Schmidt's (1958) continuum of leadership behavior to illustrate a continuum along which principal leadership decreases as teacher leadership increases. Owens and Valesky drew a diagram of "continuum of leadership behavior," with one end of the continuum being "area of freedom for principals" and the other "area of freedom for teacher." On the one end, "Principal makes decision that teachers accept"; on the other end, "Principal and teachers jointly make decision within limits defined by organizational constraints"; between the two ends, the principal's leadership decreases and teachers' leadership increases.

Similar observations consistent with the zero-sum game theory are frequently made. For example, the following sentiments were uncovered by researchers based on their research: (a) teacher professionalism is treated as an antithetical concept to principal leadership (Sergiovanni, 1992; Shantz & Pruieur, 1996); (b) principals complain that teacher empowerment reduces their power (Blasé & Kirby, 2008); and (c) various structures, such as site-based management councils, school improvement teams, leadership councils, etc., cast leadership as a shared but zero-sum phenomenon (Malen & Cochran, 2008).

The zero-sum game theory is also manifested in educational practice and policy. Fowler (2009) observed that since 1831 educational reformers had gradually established bureaucracies at both state and district levels and further in schools where the roles of principals and teachers were gradually differentiated. As a result, decision-making in schools is carefully allocated: decisions about classroom policy – what to teach, how to use time, and how to assess progress – are traditionally made by teachers, other decisions that affect teachers' work – scheduling, class placement, assignment of specialists, and the allocation of budget and materials – are made by principals (Boles & Troen, 1994; Johnson & Short, 1998). Boles and Troen (1994) assert that, this norm, in which teachers feel powerless to affect schoolwide policy, is widely accepted by teachers and administrators, and this view of power as a "zero-sum game" makes it difficult for teacher leaders to emerge in schools. The traditional figuration of leadership distribution assumes that the amount of leadership is finite, and policies, such as 2002 No Child Left Behind (NCLB), have begun to challenge the traditional figuration.

New policies are usually viewed as a way of redistributing leadership. For instance, one of the criticisms of No Child Left Behind (NCLB) is that leadership is taken away from teachers and local school districts and redistributed to the federal level, resulting in new educational federalism (Gordon et al., 2008; Jackson et al., 2021; Lewis, 2002; McDermott & Jensen, 2005; McGuinn, 2005; Shores & Steinberg, 2022; Sunderman & Kim, 2007).

EXPANDABLE POWER PIE AND THE WIN-WIN SITUATION

While the theory of zero-sum game focuses on the size of pieces cut from the fixed leadership pie, the theory of win-win situation emphasizes the creation of "a bigger pie" to benefit actors involved in the decision-making (Rux, 1998). In a win-win situation, the leadership pie is not fixed but expandable. Kouzes and Posner (1987) concur with this view by stating the following: "the expandable power pie concept leads to greater reciprocity of influence – the leader and the follower are willing to be mutually influenced by one another." (p. 164) Kanter proposed a similar idea in her seminal article published in *Harvard Business Review* in 1979. Entitling one of the sections "To expand power, share it," she urged leaders to share leadership responsibilities and argued that when a leader shares, the amount of leadership grows (Kanter, 1994).

Unlike the zero-sum game theory, positive impacts of the theory of win-win situations were reported by various researchers. For instance,

Shantz and Pruieur (1996) found that leaders who employ collaborative strategies and strive to facilitate leadership qualities in others enhance the development of teacher professionalism. Blasé and Blasé (2001) found that when principals effectively practice shared leadership, they did more than "share power" – they "multiplied" it and produced greater capacity and leadership density in their schools. Ingersoll (2003) inquired into the zero-sum game assumption between organizational control and employee control, and found that "nothing in my research suggests this to be the case. To the contrary, the data analysis ... shows that increasing the control wielded by teachers has a positive effect on relations between teachers and administrators" (p. 245).

As early as 1973, Sergiovanni and Carver argued that school leaders do not automatically lose leadership as teachers gain influence: "There is no fixed power pie to be distributed – power distribution is not necessarily a win-lose proposition" (p. 102). Sergiovanni and Carver suggested an open system in the school which permits leadership expansion. That is, if actor A increases its leadership, the total amount of leadership for the school increases – permitting not only A's leadership expansion, but the expansion of other actors' leadership as well. This relationship suggests that gains in teacher leadership potentially increase the leadership of school administrators as well. As Barth (1990) observes, when teachers are enlisted and empowered as school leaders, everyone can win: "Other teachers' concerns are frequently better understood by one of their fellows ... and the principal wins by recognizing that there is plenty of leadership to go around ... Leadership is not a zero-sum game" (p. 128).

THE NEED FOR EMPIRICAL STUDIES ON THE THEORIES OF WIN-WIN SITUATION AND ZERO-SUM GAME

The previous two sections on the theories of win-win situation and zero-sum game indicate that both theories have their supporters. As a whole, the literature has several major limitations. First, in the literature, these theories are often proposed as theoretical hypotheses and philosophically polarized stances. As noted by Katzenmeyer and Moller (2009), these theories were rarely examined empirically. Therefore, we urgently need empirical studies to test the validity of these theories as they have significant implications for the education and practice of teachers, principals, superintendents, and others. In the literature, we have empirical studies on (a) how principals and teachers perceived their own power and how principals perceived teachers' power (Keiser & Shen, 2000; Shen, 2001) and (b) conceptions of leadership and power held by teachers and principals (Hsieh & Shen, 1998; Rodriguez-Campos et al., 2008). However, studies that examine the relationship between teacher leadership and principal leadership in the context of "win-win" and "zero-sum" theories are rare.

Second, the literature fails to specify leadership domains, such as establishing curriculum and determining the school budget, in which a win-win situation or a zero-sum game occurs. Without differentiating various leadership areas in the K-12 setting which ranges from classroom practice to school budget, the one-size-fits-all approach in the literature – that tends to propose either the theory of a win-win situation or the zero-sum game theory in general terms – might oversimplify the situation. Based on Ingersoll's (1994) and Shen's (2001) studies that indicate the variation of principals' and teachers' influence on or control in various areas, the leadership relationship between principals and teachers might depend on the areas.

Third, the literature review also indicates that school level is usually a moderating variable (e.g., Angelle & Schmid, 2007; Muijs & Harris, 2003; Southworth, 2002; Stone et al., 1997; Wahlstrom & Louis, 2008; York-Barr & Duke, 2004). There are consistent patterns of difference in organizational structure and school culture between the elementary and secondary levels. The leadership relationship could vary between the elementary and secondary levels.

Finally, the practice of preparation and selection of school principals in the US also provides an impetus for the study. In many countries around the world, there is no formal training for school principals, and school principals are promoted from the teacher ranks. However, the US has a long history of having preparation programs for school principals, and the preparation is usually at the master's level, including courses such as leadership theory, school law, budgeting, supervision, principalship, and school-community relations. A building-level certificate is typically required for being a principal in the US (Shen et al., 2005). Therefore, the situation in the US provides a unique context for studying the leadership relationship between teachers and principals.

EMPIRICAL STUDIES ON THE RELATIONSHIP BETWEEN PRINCIPAL AND TEACHER LEADERSHIP

Study 1. Relationship between Principal and Teacher Leadership in Traditional Public Schools in the US

The Schools and Staffing Survey (SASS) 1999–2000 was used to conduct this study (Shen & Xia, 2012). SASS was an appropriate dataset for the study because of the following: first, it is a nationally representative survey, from which the findings could be generalized to the national level. Second, its richness of variables allowed controlling teacher- and school-level characteristics, which might affect the relationship. Third, the fact that teachers were nested within principals/schools and the sample size was large gave the methodological advantage to use multilevel modeling to model the relationship between principal and teacher leadership at two different levels. The sample included 42,086 teachers and 8,524 principals in traditional public schools. Among others, the survey asked principals and teachers to rate their level of influence in the seven leadership domains ("set performance standards," "establish curriculum," "determine the content of in-service professional development programs," "hire new full-time teachers," "evaluate teachers," "set discipline policy," and "decide how the school budget is spent"). The study tested empirically if the relationship between principal and teacher leadership was characterized by a win-win situation or a zero-sum game.

The findings indicated that among the seven domains we investigated, the leadership relationship between principals and teachers was statistically significant and positive in six domains (i.e., "set performance standards," "establish curriculum," "determine the content of in-service professional development programs," "hire new full-time teachers," "set discipline policy," and "decide how the school budget is spent"), suggesting that the leadership relationship between principals and teachers in these domains was characterized by the win-win theory. However, in the domain of "evaluate teachers," the relationship was statistically significant and negative, indicating the relation was characterized by the zero-sum game theory in the domain of "evaluate teachers." Although both the win-win theory and the zero-sum game theory seemed to have some empirical supporting evidence for various leadership domains, the leadership relationship between teachers and principals was characterized predominantly by the win-win theory, with the zero-sum game theory only applying to one domain.

In the six areas, where the relationship was characterized by the win-win theory, the level of the win-win situations varied slightly. The following list was arranged from the lowest to the highest level of win-win situations: "set performance standards," "determine the content of professional development," "set discipline policy," "establish curriculum," "decide how to spend school budget," and "hire new full-time teachers." It appears that the level of win-win situation was higher in domains where traditionally principals play a bigger role, such as "decide how to spend school budget."

The literature indicates that there could be a difference between the elementary and secondary levels in leadership, school culture, and other areas. Therefore, we split the sample into elementary and secondary levels and conducted two sets of analyses for the elementary and secondary levels, respectively. The results comparing elementary and secondary schools in the relationship between the principal and the teacher leadership revealed that as far as the seven domains were concerned, the leadership relationship characterized by the win-win theory was more prevalent at the elementary level than at the secondary level. In other words, we would be more likely to see the win-win situation in leadership relationships at the elementary level than at the secondary level.

Study 2. Relationship between Principal and Teacher Leadership in the US Revisited

We revisited the topic of the relationship between principal and teacher leadership in the US by using the SASS 2011–2012, data collected twelve years later than the first study (Xia & Shen, 2020). Given the development of charter schools, for the second study the sample consisted of both traditional public schools and charter schools to capture the whole picture for public schools. The sample consisted of 7,510 public school principals and 37,500 public school teachers, representing 89,810 public school principals and 3,385,170 public school teachers. The key survey items for leadership domains were identical to the ones used in the first study.

For the whole sample, the results were very similar to those based on the data collected twelve years earlier. After controlling for both teacher and school/principal characteristics, in six leadership domains (all except for "evaluate teachers") principal leadership showed statistically significant and positive associations with corresponding teacher leadership. This indicated that among the six leadership domains, when principals' actual influence was high, teachers' actual influence was high as well, indicating a win-win situation of leadership relationship.

"Evaluate teachers" was a unique leadership area in which the principal leadership showed a negative but not significant association with teacher leadership. This indicated that for this leadership domain, there was no clear pattern on the relationship between principal and teacher leadership, implying neither a win-win situation nor a zero-sum game.

Further examination of the findings showed that for the six leadership domains characterized by the win-win situation, their strengths could be categorized into three groups. The strongest win-win leadership relationship existed in the areas of "hire new full-time teachers" and "establish curriculum." The medium win-win leadership relationships occurred in the domains of "setting discipline policy," "decide the content of professional development," and "decide how to spend school budget." The weakest win-win leadership relationship lay in the domain of "set performance standards."

As for the comparison between the elementary and secondary levels, the results indicated that for both elementary and secondary schools, there was a statistically significant, positive relationship between principal and teacher leadership in six same policy areas ("set performance standards," "establish curriculum," "determine content of professional development," "hire new full-time teachers," "set discipline policy," and "decide how to spend school budget"). This finding was different from the first study based on 1999–2000 in which we found that for elementary schools, there was a statistically significant, positive relationship between the principal and teacher power in five areas ("establish curriculum," "determine content of professional development," "hire new full-time teachers," "set discipline policy," and "decide how to spend school budget"), while for secondary schools, there was a statistically significant, positive relationship between the principal and teacher leadership in two domains ("hire new full-time teachers" and "decide how to spend school budget"). In other words, the relationship between principal and teacher leadership was characterized by the win-win situation more in 2011–2012 than in 1999–2000, particularly at the secondary level.

For the six leadership domains that were characterized as win-win situations, although the estimated leadership relationship coefficients in the corresponding leadership areas were always larger for elementary schools than those for secondary schools, their confidence intervals indicated that there were no statistically significant differences in five domains. The only exception was the area of "establish curriculum": where the difference was marginally significant. This finding was consistent with the first study. The result seemed to suggest that, like twelve years ago, as far as "establish curriculum" is concerned, the power relationship between teachers and principals was still more characterized by the win-win theory at the elementary level than at the secondary level.

Finally, as in the whole sample, "evaluate teachers" was the only domain where there was a negative but statistically non-significant relationship between teachers' and principals' power for both elementary and secondary schools. This finding was also similar to the results of the first study. It seemed to suggest that, like twelve years ago, evaluating teachers was still a unique area and that the power relationship between teachers and principals was neither a win-win situation nor a zero-sum game.

As to the comparison between charter and non-charter schools, the results indicated that for charter schools there was a statistically significant, positive relationship between the principal and teacher leadership in six leadership domains ("set performance standards," "establish curriculum," "determine content of professional development," "hire new full-time teachers," "set discipline policy," and "decide how to spend school budget"), while for non-charter public schools, there was a statistically significant, positive relationship between the principal and teacher leadership in four domains ("set performance standards," "establish curriculum," "determine content of professional development," and "decide how to spend school budget"). It seems that as far as the seven domains were concerned, the leadership relationship characterized by the win-win theory was slightly more prevalent in charter schools than in the non-charter public schools. In charter schools, principal and teacher leadership had a statistically significant, negative relationship for the domain of "evaluate teachers," signaling that the leadership relationship was characterized by zero-sum in this particular domain. In non-charter public schools, there was a positive, but statistically not significant relationship between principal and teacher leadership in the area of "evaluate teachers" and "hire teachers"; for "set discipline policy," the relationship between principal and teacher leadership was negative and close to zero; the results indicated that in traditional public schools, there was no clear pattern for either a win-win situation or a zero-sum game for these three domains.

THE FEASIBILITY, PREVALENCE, AND IMPLICATIONS OF THE WIN-WIN SITUATION

The results from the two earlier studies based on national datasets collected at two different times generally demonstrate that the relationship between principal and teacher leadership is characterized by the win-win theory. The studies have implications for both theory and practice. First, the feasibility of the win-win theory is confirmed by empirical studies. The results clearly demonstrate that the win-win theory is possible. It supports the hypothesis that the amount of leadership could be expanded, resulting in a win-win situation (e.g., Covey, 1989; Kanter, 1994; Kouzes & Posner, 1987).

Second, the empirical studies indicate that the win-win theory is prevalent in practice. As far as the whole samples are concerned, the relationship between principal and teacher leadership is characterized in six out of seven areas of leadership domains. There has been an ideological war between the win-win theory and the zero-sum game theory for many years. The win-win theory has been proposed as an ideal model, with little empirical evidence. The two empirical studies demonstrate that the practice characterized by the win-win theory is prevalent in many leadership domains.

Third, the feasibility and prevalence of the win-win theory in the public school system offers a new perspective on school improvement. In the literature, there have been arguments for the effects of principal and teacher leadership on school outcomes. For example, there have been literature reviews and meta-analyses of the effect of principal leadership (Shen & Wu, 2024; Wu & Shen, 2022) and teacher leadership (Shen et al., 2020; Tan et al., 2024; York-Barr & Duke, 2004), respectively, on student achievement, quantifying the effects of principal leadership and teacher leadership. The research on principal leadership and teacher leadership has yielded much knowledge for improving school practice and outcomes. However, generally speaking, principal leadership and teacher leadership have been considered in a parallel fashion (Campbell et al., 2018; Datnow & Park, 2018; Harris et al., 2017). Given the finding that the relationship between principal and teacher leadership is characterized predominantly by the win-win situation, it is logical to emphasize, for the purpose of school improvement, not only principal and teacher leadership on their own, but also the relationship between them. Since the relationship between principal and teacher leadership is characterized by the win-win theory, principal and teacher leadership could enhance each other, and as a result, increase the overall leadership density in schools.

Finally, the win-win situation for principal and teacher leadership points to the feasibility and importance of harnessing the power of principal leadership and teacher leadership for school improvement, particularly in the context of the theory of the bifurcated educational system. As discussed in Chapter 2, there is a fault line between the state-district-school tectonic plate and the classroom tectonic plate. Bridging the fault line plays an extremely important role in bettering the efforts of school improvement (Shen, 2020). The win-win situation, supported by the empirical findings, makes it both feasible to utilize leadership (i.e., principal leadership and teacher leadership) to bridge the fault and imperative to do so. In Chapter 4, we will discuss a framework for integrated learning-centered school leadership with a focus on the "content" of school renewal.

Integrated Learning-Centered School Leadership

A Framework of "Content" of School Renewal

INTRODUCTION

Considerable literature recognizes principal leadership and teacher leadership as playing important roles in the academic success of students and schools. Nonetheless, the literature tends to treat principal leadership and teacher leadership in a separate manner. Very rarely is the focus on the integration of principal leadership and teacher leadership, which can be referred to as integrated or collective school leadership. As a result, even though there are a number of instruments measuring either principal leadership or teacher leadership, there is essentially no instrument that measures integrated school leadership. We aim to help fill this void via our present study. Specifically, our goal was to develop and validate an instrument that researchers can use to measure the collective effort of principals and teachers who exercise their own unique leadership to generate integrated school leadership. Apart from the psychometric validation of this instrument, we also aim to explore the predictive properties of this instrument in predicting academic achievement at the school level, such as a school's percentage of students who reach the proficiency level in core content areas such as mathematics and reading.

MOVING TOWARD INTEGRATED SCHOOL LEADERSHIP

The literature on educational leadership is dominated by the concepts of principal leadership and teacher leadership, but researchers often discuss principal leadership and teacher leadership in isolation as if, in the presence of one, the other were absent in the context of school management and operation. This limitation highlights itself given the classic finding that the impacts of principal leadership on school success tend to be indirect through teachers, particularly concerning student achievement (e.g., Dutta & Sahney, 2016; Hallinger & Heck, 1996a, 1996b, 1998; Leithwood & Jantzi, 2000). There is a need to integrate principal leadership and teacher leadership into a new general concept of school leadership for the improvement of students and schools. To inquire into such a concept, we review the literature on principal leadership and teacher leadership first and then conceptualize school leadership.

Principal Leadership

The inquiry into principal leadership has gone through three main stages, moving from specific leadership traits or behaviors to certain types of leadership models to more pragmatic and balanced leadership that embodies a more comprehensive list of leadership traits, behaviors, and dispositions. The first stage spanned mostly the 1980s and 1990s with a focus on the description of principals' traits, behaviors, strategies, and effects as educational leaders. For example, Eberts and Stone (1988) found that conflict resolution was an effective trait of principals that directly and significantly improved student achievement. Brewer (1993) reported that the work of principals on teacher selection and goal setting is positively and significantly related to schooling outcomes. Friedkin and Slater (1994) discovered that students perform better academically in schools where principals play the role of teachers' advisors.

The inquiry into various leadership traits and behaviors of principals made it possible for the theories on principal leadership style to thrive. The second stage witnessed the birth of several leadership models that essentially categorize leadership traits and behaviors of principals. Major principal leadership models include transformational leadership (e.g., Boberg & Bourgeois, 2016; Hallinger, 2003; Leithwood & Jantzi, 2005, 2006; Marks & Printy, 2003; Rafferty & Griffin, 2004), instructional leadership (e.g., Blase & Blase, 1999, 2000; Hallinger, 2003; Marks & Printy, 2003; O'Donnell & White, 2005; Shatzer et al., 2013), collegial leadership (e.g., Little, 1985; Marks & Louis, 1997; Sweetland & Hoy, 2000), and distributed leadership (e.g., Chang, 2011; Louis et al., 2010; Mangin, 2005;

Spillane, 2006; Spillane et al., 2001; Hallinger & Heck, 2010a, 2010b; Heck & Hallinger, 2009).

During this stage, many studies also attempted to compare and connect leadership models. For example, Robinson et al. (2008) suggested that instructional leadership is more effective than transformational leadership in terms of improving schooling outcomes. Hallinger (2003) advocated combining the two models (theories) given the commonalities and differences between transformational leadership and instructional leadership. Marks and Printy (2003) supported such an effort, arguing that transformational leadership does not carry much practical educational information.

The second stage evolved gradually into a recognition by many researchers that the work of principals as educational leaders is too complicated to be simply categorized into a number of leadership models. For example, Leithwood et al. (2004) expressed their concern about the "leadership by adjective" literature (p. 6), arguing that "sometimes these adjectives have real meaning, but sometimes they mask the more important underlying themes common to successful leadership, regardless of the style being advocated" (p. 6). Likewise, Hallinger and Heck (1998) as well as Witziers et al. (2003) cautioned that the conceptualization of effective leadership is oversimplified in many cases. According to Shen et al. (2005), one main shortcoming of the previous paradigms on principal leadership preparation is the overwhelming focus on general leadership characteristics and management functions, thus overlooking leadership behaviors related to schooling outcomes, particularly student achievement. Leithwood and Sun (2012) advocated a shift of theoretical focus from "the exclusive use of whole leadership models" to a purposeful assembly of leadership qualities that target "more specific [educational] practices" (p. 412).

The third stage began then to search for a more comprehensive list of leadership traits, behaviors, and dispositions of principals that can improve school effectiveness (promote student achievement) instead of focusing on leadership models and styles of principals. Based on the empirical findings from the Chicago school reform between 1990 and 1996, Sebring and Bryk (2000) identified four leadership styles and four leadership strategies from effective principals. The four styles included inclusive and facilitative orientation, institutional focus on student learning, efficient management, and support and pressure that catalyze initiatives and enable teachers. The four strategies included short-term focus ("quick hits") to build agency (Sebring & Bryk, 2000, p. 2); long-term focus on instructional core; strategic orientation for clear vision, monitoring of what is working and what is not, provision of feedback for next steps; and attack "incoherence" with follow-up efforts to make sure the new initiatives succeed (Sebring & Bryk, 2000, p. 3). Leithwood et al. (2004) identified three core leadership practices that characterize effective principals, including setting directions, developing (equipping) people, and redesigning the organization. They also stated that, beyond those three basic cores, principals need a good understanding of various educational contexts for adaptation from organizational context to student population to educational policy context and for an effective response to different contextual issues. Marzano et al. (2005) developed twenty-one responsibilities for effective principal leadership that can substantially improve student achievement, reporting an average correlation of .25 between principals' overall leadership scores in those responsibilities and students' academic achievement scores.

Although many studies suggest various leadership frameworks, dimensions, and practices of effective principals, few of them provide instruments to measure principal leadership. In response, Vanderbilt Assessment of Leadership in Education (VAL-ED) was developed as a reliable and valid measure of effective principal leadership, based on empirical evidence and theoretical background. It contains six core components referred to as "characteristics of schools that support the learning of students and enhance the ability of teachers to teach" and six key processes referred to as "how leaders create and manage those core components" (Porter et al., 2010, p. 137). The combination of components and processes results in a total of 36 cells of leadership practices. Currently, the Professional Standards for Educational Leaders provides a good way to develop instruments to measure principal leadership, with ten standards and numerous sub-standards under each one (National Policy Board for Educational Administration, 2015).

Teacher Leadership

The influence of educational leadership could be greatly limited if principals were viewed as the solo leaders in school. Spillane et al. (2001)

claimed that "the prevailing framework of individual agency, focused on positional leaders such as principals, is inadequate because leadership is not just a function of what these leaders know and do" (p. 23). Sergiovanni (2005) stated that "viewing leadership as a group activity linked to practice rather than just an individual activity linked to a person helps match the expertise we have in a school with the problems we face" (p. 45). Much of the research evidence concerning effective principal leadership points to the importance of teachers working in a professional environment. For example, a series of studies by Hallinger and Heck (1996a, 1996b, 1998, 2010a, 2010b) has long highlighted the critical interaction between school leaders and key characters working in their organizational environment.

Compared to the traditional top-down leadership that focuses exclusively on principals, teacher leadership suggests an alternative bottom-up leadership that focuses on teachers. The concept of teacher leadership is developed based on the notion that "teachers are increasingly assuming more leadership functions at both the instructional and organizational levels" (Harris, 2005, p. 203). The concept of teacher leadership is promising because it views all teachers as leaders, as Fullan (1994) argued that "teacher leadership is not for a few; it is for all" (p. 115).

While the concept of principal leadership is widely accepted and reasonably developed, the concept of teacher leadership is not yet well-defined and in many cases is used as an umbrella term (Harris, 2005; York-Barr & Duke, 2004). Hanuscin et al. (2014) emphasized the need and challenge of redefining the role and rethinking the identity of teacher leadership. The difficulty comes perhaps from the fact that the concept of teacher leadership intersects many other important leadership concepts such as distributive leadership (Muijs & Harris, 2003), professional development (Darling-Hammond et al., 1995), professionalization of teaching (Murphy, 2005), and professional learning communities (York-Barr & Duke, 2004).

Silva et al. (2002) concluded that there are three approaches to understand the leadership roles of teachers. In the first approach, teacher leaders are understood as head teachers or department heads who act like "managers" to focus only on the efficiency of the schooling system. In the second approach, teacher leaders are viewed as curriculum experts and instructional leaders. Nonetheless, their leadership is often confined to a classroom (a teacher's daily work). In the third approach, teacher leaders become re-designers (educational reformers) and agents (cultural changers) exercising their influence on the "goals, structure, roles, and norms of an organization" (p. 781). In other words, teacher leaders are now considered having critical influence on all aspects of schooling.

Much of the literature on teacher leadership highlights the first and second approaches, that is, emphasizing teacher leaders' role in curriculum and instruction, because teachers tend to feel more comfortable with their role inside the classroom (curriculum and instruction) than outside the classroom (lack of sufficient training to act) (Handler, 2010). The lack of support is another reason why teachers are reluctant to become change agents for the whole school. For example, Nolan and Palazzolo (2012) found that novice teachers have the desire to get involved in decision-making on curriculum and instruction at the school level, but schools do not provide them with opportunities to make really meaningful decisions.

Finally, some voices question the concept of teacher leadership. For example, Leithwood and Jantzi (2000) studied the effects of principal leadership and teacher leadership on student engagement. They found significant (though weak) effects of principal leadership but insignificant effects of teacher leadership. They eventually argued that "grafting the concept of leadership onto the concept of teacher" may not make a significant contribution to school effectiveness and improvement (p. 430).

School Leadership as Integrated Leadership

It is obvious in the literature that existing theories and models of principal leadership and teacher leadership are developed separately. Most studies tend to focus on one and ignore the other. When leadership is measured separately between principals and teachers, the compounding effects of principal leadership and teacher leadership are difficult to estimate (Leithwood & Jantzi, 1999, 2000). Crowther et al. (2002) developed the concept of parallel leadership in order to address the inseparable nature of principal leadership and teacher leadership. They defined parallel leadership as "a process whereby teacher leaders and their principals engage in collective action to build school capacity" which "embodies mutual respect, shared purpose, and allowance for individual expression" (Crowther et al., 2002, p. 38).

Based on a series of research syntheses, Hallinger and Heck (1996a, 1996b, 1998, 2010a, 2010b, 2011) proposed a comprehensive conceptual framework for leadership effectiveness. Essentially, they sorted empirical findings concerning effective principals into three types of conceptualization on school leadership, including the direct-effects model (teachers do not interact with principals), the mediated-effects model (teachers passively mediate principals), and the reciprocal-effects model (teachers actually interact with principals). They argued that while the mediated-effects model outweighs the direct-effects model in terms of capturing the indirect effects of principals, the mediated-effects model still understates the organization's overall environmental effects, thus oversimplifying the educational process of how principals can impact student learning. Heck and Hallinger (2010) suggested the reciprocal-effects model to account for the interaction between principal leadership and teacher leadership. This model highlights collaborative leadership that establishes school structures and processes to strengthen "shared commitment to achieving school improvement goals, broad participation and collaboration in decision making, and shared accountability for student learning outcomes" (Heck & Hallinger, 2010, p. 228).

In general, we are in line with the literature that emphasizes the interaction between principal leadership and teacher leadership, and we specifically argue that the literature contains sufficient evidence to explicitly refer to the leadership dynamics within the "walls" of a school as an integration of principal leadership and teacher leadership. Such a "gentle" step in the literature closes many gaps and creates many opportunities in measurement and evaluation. One of the benefits of seeing school leadership as integrated leadership is that researchers can combine (team up) principals and teachers as one force or party that aims to improve school success and student achievement, with credits and criticisms to be shared between the two groups (shared accountability). We therefore argue for the need for research on this more collective concept of school leadership. Based on such a need is our justification to develop and validate an instrument that measures integrated school leadership.

Indeed, the complex interaction between principal leadership and teacher leadership on student achievement has rarely been discussed in the literature. One initiative along this line of research is to distill the dimensions of integrated school leadership, and a part of this effort is to develop an instrument that measures school leadership from the perspective of the integration between principal leadership and teacher leadership. Shen and colleagues have begun to map out the dimensions of school leadership based on comprehensive reviews of literature (Shen et al., 2013; Shen et al., 2015; Shen & Cooley, 2012). They suggested seven dimensions to understand school leadership, including data-informed decision-making; safe and orderly school operation; high, cohesive, and culturally relevant expectations for all students; distributive and empowering leadership; coherent curriculum; real-time and embedded instructional assessment; and commitment and passion for school renewal. It is the goal of the current study to develop and validate an instrument based on this conceptualization of school leadership.

THE BACKGROUND OF THE STUDY

Data

Data were collected from a professional development project at Western Michigan University in collaboration with the Michigan Association of Secondary School Principals and the Michigan Elementary and Middle School Principals Associations. Principals who were members of those associations were invited to participate in the project, and fifty-three principals responded to our invitation. Teachers from their schools were then invited to take part in the project, and 644 teachers responded to our invitation. Teachers were administered the instrument we developed to measure integrated school leadership, and then such data were used to conduct the validation part of our study ($N = 644$).

For the prediction part of our study, in which we attempted to explore whether our instrument is able to predict student achievement at the school level, teacher responses were merged with school performance and background data. Because schools were the unit of analysis in the prediction part of our study, responses from teachers on the instrument were aggregated to the school level. Finally, because we needed to connect teachers with schools, four teachers without school identification were removed from the prediction part of our study, reducing the number of teachers to 640. After aggregation, those teachers were matched with the fifty-three schools (principals) ($N = 53$).

Measures

The Teacher Survey on Learning-Centered School Leadership is our instrument, which comprises forty-two items forming seven scales (see Appendix 4.1). Construct validity of this instrument was established based on a comprehensive review of the literature. Seven scales (factors) were identified from the literature review, and a team of researchers and experienced practitioners identified six major discrete behaviors under each scale drawing as much evidence as possible from the literature. These discrete behaviors led to the construction of items (statements) as seen in Appendix 4.1. We expect teachers to be fairly familiar with these statements because they encounter issues associated with those statements on a daily basis in their teaching.

In using the instrument, teachers were instructed to choose one option that corresponds the most to their perception on each statement that portrays integrated school leadership. Options for each statement include 1 = strongly disagree, 2 = moderately disagree, 3 = slightly disagree, 4 = slightly agree, 5 = moderately agree, and 6 = strongly agree. All items were constructed positively so that a higher response demonstrates stronger integrated school leadership. Reliability statistics ranged from .85 to .92 for scales, with an overall reliability coefficient of .97 for the instrument.

Student achievement data came from the Michigan Educational Assessment Program (MEAP). The Michigan Statewide Assessment Selection Guidelines mandated this state assessment for students in Grades 3 to 8 and 11 (Michigan Department of Education [MDE], 2011, p. B-2). MEAP is a content-based assessment aligned directly to the statewide content standards referred to as Grade Level Content Expectations and demonstrates good psychometric properties (MDE, 2006, p. 154). Although individual students' MEAP scores were not available, we obtained the proportion of students in each school whose MEAP scores reached the proficient level in each of two core content areas: mathematics and reading (English). These proportions were measures of student achievement at the school level.

We also collected critical contextual information for each participating school from the school's website. School contextual variables included school (enrollment) size, percentage of male students (measuring school gender composition), percentage of White students (measuring school racial–ethnic composition), and percentage of students eligible for free lunch (measuring school socioeconomic composition). We used these school contextual variables to adjust for student achievement measures at the school level. All measures at the school level were obtained for 2015 in this study.

Analysis

To conduct the validation part of the study, we performed confirmatory factor analysis (CFA) to examine whether the seven-factor structure that we identified through the review of the literature was able to fit the collected teacher response data. We had a sufficient sample size of 644 to perform a credible CFA, based on the suggestion of a minimum sample size between 100 and 200 (MacCallum et al., 1999). Procedurally, we compared the seven-factor structure with both the baseline structure (referred to as the null structure with no factor) and the single-factor structure (referred to as the general structure with a unitary definition or concept of school leadership). Please see Figures A.4.2.1 and A.4.2.2 for the one- and seven-factor models in Appendix 4.2. Comparison of the hypothesized structure with the baseline and one-factor structures is a routine procedure in instrument validation.

Model-data-fit statistics are the primary evidence in instrument validity. We applied multiple measures of model-data fit as a way to cross-validate the seven-factor structure. The χ^2 test offers an overall fit of the data to the structure, with a smaller χ^2 value indicating a better fit. The χ^2 statistic is sensitive to sample size, model size, and variable distribution. The standardized root mean square residual (SRMR) is another measure, with a value smaller than .08 as a good fit (Hu & Bentler, 1999). The comparative fit index (CFI) avoids the underestimation of the model-data fit that tends to occur with a small sample. The Tucker-Lewis index (TLI) is a model-data-fit measure that is independent of sample size. Both CFI and TLI measure the proportion of variance explained in relation to the null model, with a value greater than .90 as a good fit (Hu & Bentler,

1999). To understand the measurement properties of the instrument, we performed reliability analysis (Cronbach's alpha) to ensure the internal consistency of each scale and the instrument as a whole are acceptable. In addition, we examined skewness to ensure that scores are roughly symmetrical around the mean and kurtosis to ensure that the distributions are neither overly peaked nor overly flat.

To conduct the prediction part of the study, we performed multiple regression analyses with school as the unit of analysis. We conducted the regression analyses for mathematics and reading in a separate manner. For each content area, we used the proportion of students within a school whose MEAP scores reached the proficient level as the dependent variable, and we used response scores of each scale of the instrument and the instrument as a whole as the predictor variables (independent variables) also in a separate manner. This allowed us to examine the predictive properties of each scale of the instrument and the instrument as a whole. When running the regression models, we used school contextual variables as the control variables so that the ability of each scale of the instrument and the instrument as a whole to predict a school's proportion of proficient students was adjusted for the contextual characteristics of the school.

WHAT WE FOUND

With the instrument presented in Appendix 4.1, we calculate descriptive statistics about our data (see Appendix 4.3). The current study contained two parts whose analysis was based on different data. The validation part of the study used teachers as the unit of analysis to perform CFA ($N = 644$), and the prediction part of the study used schools as the unit of analysis to perform regression analyses ($N = 53$). Appendix 4.3 presents the descriptive statistics of the background variables for our regression analyses. Similar to many validation studies in the literature, descriptive statistics at the item level (for CFA) were omitted for the sake of space.

Validation of the Instrument

With data from the forty-two items on the instrument arranged into a seven-factor structure, we performed CFA to examine the perception of

Table 4.1 *Model-data-fit indices (N = 644)*

Model	χ^2	CFI	TLI	SRMR
Null model	19523.81	–	–	–
One-factor model	5808.89	0.73	0.72	0.07
Seven-factor model	3152.18	0.87	0.86	0.06

Note: CFI = comparative fit index; TLI = Tucker-Lewis index; SRMR = standardized root mean square residual.

teachers on integrated school leadership. Table 4.1 presents the results of model-data fit that measure the extent to which the seven-factor structure fits our data. We reiterate that model-data-fit of the seven-factor structure was examined in comparison with the baseline and single-factor structures. Comparatively, the seven-factor structure improved the model-data fit dramatically over the baseline and single-factor structures. Specifically, we found a substantial decrease in the χ^2 statistic when comparing the seven-factor structure with the single-factor structure and in particular with the baseline structure. The seven-factor structure improved over the single-factor structure in terms of SRMR, with a value (.06) well below .08. Although neither CFI nor TLI went beyond .90, their respective values of .87 and .86 were reasonably close to the threshold. Furthermore, both CFI and TLI clearly favored the seven-factor structure over the single-factor structure. Overall, the results of the model-data fit confirmed from multiple perspectives that the specification of items on the instrument was supported by our data. In other words, items measured factors they were proposed to measure (e.g., the first six items on the instrument were loaded onto the factor of data-informed decision-making as we proposed or expected).

With the seven-factor structure identified as our final structure representing teachers' perception of integrated school leadership, we sought to establish some basic psychometric properties of each scale of the instrument and the instrument as a whole (see Table 4.2). The routine reliability analysis indicated strong internal consistency across scales of the instrument (from .85 to .92) and the instrument as a whole (.97). Therefore, all scales of the instrument and, particularly, the instrument as a whole were reliable. We also examined the distribution of scores for

Table 4.2 *Measurement properties of the instrument*

	Alpha	Skewness	Kurtosis
Data-informed decision-making	.85	−.23	−.06
Safe and orderly school operation	.88	−.32	.45
High, cohesive, and culturally relevant expectations for all students	.88	.39	1.00
Distributive and empowering leadership	.88	−.19	−.35
Coherent curricular programs	.92	−.16	−.08
Real-time and embedded instructional assessment	.90	−.07	−.78
Commitment and passion for school renewal	.91	−.32	−.19
Total	.97	−.05	−.26

each scale of the instrument and the instrument as a whole, based on skewness and kurtosis, the most commonly used indicators for distributional properties. Given that the values of skewness and kurtosis between −2.00 and 2.00 are usually considered acceptable for a univariate normal distribution (George & Mallery, 2010), our analytical results on skewness and kurtosis did not raise any concerns about the distribution of scores for any scale on the instrument and the instrument as a whole. Overall, the validation results provided strong evidence supporting the instrument's factorial validity and reliability.

Prediction of the Instrument

Given that the ultimate educational goal of integrated school leadership is to improve student achievement, we attempted to examine how well the instrument that measures school leadership can predict student achievement at the school level. Table 4.3 presents the results of the instrument predicting the (within-school) proportion of students who performed at the proficient level in mathematics and reading, respectively. The instrument as a whole significantly predicted the proportion of students at the proficient level in both mathematics and reading. As to individual scales of the instrument, three out of seven significantly predicted student achievement in both mathematics and reading (high, cohesive, and culturally relevant expectations for all students; coherent curricular

Table 4.3 *Analytical results of instrument and its components making prediction of school percentage of students at proficient level in academic achievement*

Component	Effect	SE	R^2
Data-informed decision-making			
Mathematics	7.07*	3.29	.39
Reading	5.14	3.06	.56
Safe and orderly school operation			
Mathematics	6.58*	3.07	.39
Reading	4.01	2.88	.55
High, cohesive, and culturally relevant expectations for all students			
Mathematics	11.63*	3.15	.49
Reading	7.62*	3.08	.59
Distributive and empowering leadership			
Mathematics	7.84	3.15	.41
Reading	3.81	3.08	.55
Coherent curricular programs			
Mathematics	6.37*	2.44	.42
Reading	4.43[†]	2.30	.57
Real-time and embedded instructional assessment			
Mathematics	4.37	3.58	.35
Reading	3.31	3.28	.54
Commitment and passion for school renewal			
Mathematics	9.14*	3.25	.43
Reading	6.90*	3.05	.58
Total			
Mathematics	9.77*	3.48	.43
Reading	6.47[†]	3.30	.57

Note: *p < .05. [†]p < .06. All estimates are controlled for school enrollment, percentage of male students, percentage of White students, and percentage of students eligible for free or reduced-price lunch. Adjusted R^2 is reported.

programs; commitment and passion for school renewal). In addition, two more scales successfully predicted the proportion of students at the proficient level in mathematics (data-informed decision-making, safe and orderly school operation). Finally, the remaining two scales did not predict the proportion of students at the proficient level in either mathematics or reading (distributive and empowering leadership, real-time, and embedded instructional assessment).

Table 4.3 also provides information on the adequacy (performance) of the regression model. The conventional statistic, R^2, represents the proportion of variance explained by the regression model. In the case of the instrument as a whole, 43 percent and 57 percent of the variance in the dependent variable (the within-school proportion of students who performed at the proficient level) was accounted for in mathematics and reading respectively. Values of R^2 such as those are a convincing indication that the regression model was quite adequate in making the prediction. For the scales of the instrument, R^2 ranged from .35 to .49 in mathematics and from .54 to .59 in reading. Again, these values all indicated good adequacy of the regression model. Great model performance critically increased our confidence in presenting the predictive properties of the instrument.

We noticed that many successful predictions (made by the instrument) were practically large. For example, on the measurement scale of 1–6, a one-point improvement in high, cohesive, and culturally relevant expectations for all students would increase the within-school proportion of students who perform at the proficient level in mathematics by nearly 12 percent. Please recall that the performance for each school was measured by the proportion of students within the school whose MEAP scores reached the proficient level (in mathematics and reading separately), as discussed previously. This percentage, therefore, corresponds to that proportion. Even for the smallest effects, on the measurement scale of 1–6, one-score-point improvement in coherent curricular programs would increase the proportion of students at the proficient level in reading by almost 4.5 percent. We considered such a range of improvement in student achievement at the school level very positive and promising. Overall, Table 4.3 indicates that the instrument can indeed measure the kind of integrated school leadership that really matters to student achievement.

WHAT THE FINDINGS MEAN

Integrated school leadership is a fairly recent concept of educational leadership born to address the often-seen separation between principal leadership and teacher leadership in the literature. The concept, as we discussed earlier, is theoretically important, attempting to bridge principal leadership and teacher leadership into one general shared leadership with the goal of improving student achievement. With the concept comes the challenge of measuring school leadership. We developed and validated an instrument for such a purpose in the current study. Meanwhile, we realize that any instrument that claims to measure school leadership must be able to reasonably predict student achievement (must be sensitive to student achievement) because, as we stated earlier, the ultimate educational goal of school leadership is to improve student achievement. We examined the predictability of our instrument on student achievement in the current study.

The results on the validation of the instrument indicate sound psychometric properties. The current study indicates that teachers' perceptions of school leadership fit well into the theoretical dimensions of integrated school leadership for principals and teachers to jointly carry out the leadership role for school effectiveness and improvement. Stated differently, from the perspective of teachers, the instrument captures the theoretical dimensions of school leadership. Therefore, teachers are a valid source of information on the extent to which school leadership is collectively practiced by principals and teachers.

Shen et al. (2016) discussed the notion of teachers as a potential source of information that evaluates principal leadership, based on their successful validation of an instrument used by teachers. The current study adds further credibility to the notion. Perhaps, teachers are the best educational group in a school setting to experience both principal leadership and teacher leadership as well as shared leadership between principals and teachers (see also Senge, 1990). As the frontline educators working directly with students, teachers through whom any educational leadership functions may well be the best individuals to connect any educational leadership with student achievement.

The results of the prediction of the instrument on student achievement (at the school level) come forth positive and promising. Overall, the instrument can indeed measure the kind of integrated school leadership that really matters to student achievement. A range of improvement from approximately 5 to 12 percent in the within-school proportion of students who perform at the proficient level in core content areas (mathematics and reading) is quite substantial, particularly given the available space for improving school leadership. A measurement scale of 1–6 leaves sufficient room or creates adequate opportunity for schools to move up in school leadership (compared with a measurement scale of, say, 1–4).

Earlier, it was mentioned that an instrument measuring integrated school leadership must be reasonably sensitive to student achievement, because the ultimate educational goal of school leadership is to improve student achievement. The current study indicates that the instrument is more sensitive to the core content area of mathematics than that of reading (English). In Table 4.3, the instrument as a whole, together with five out of seven scales, significantly predicted student achievement at the school level (the within-school proportion of students who performed at the proficient level in mathematics). In line with a common sense among educators, parents, and students, Table 4.3 shows that doing well in mathematics tends to be more difficult than doing well in reading. From this perspective, the instrument tends to be more sensitive to more difficult school subjects such as mathematics (showing another important measurement property). Interestingly, the predicted effects of school leadership were also consistently larger on mathematics than reading (see all statistically significant results in Table 4.3). Not only does this finding add further support to the previously discussed unique measurement property of the instrument, but also it indicates that improvement in school leadership could lead to larger improvement in student achievement (at the school level) in more difficult school subjects such as mathematics.

Although the results of the instrument's validation and prediction are quite satisfactory to us, we point out a potential methodological issue concerning the outcome (dependent) measure. As the outcome measure, the within-school proportion of students who perform at the proficient level in a core content area is closely related to the issue of standard setting (see Bejar, 2008). Because we derived one student achievement measure (at the school level) for each school, the proportion was aggregated across grade levels within the school. In Michigan, for example, an elementary school contains three state-mandated testing grade levels (Grades 3–5), and thus there are three proportions, one for each grade level, that are aggregated to produce one student achievement measure (at the school level) for the elementary school. A proportion for any grade level is established based on a cutoff score point (standard setting) that is obviously arbitrary. Because the content in, say, mathematics is different from Grades 3 to 5, the cutoff score points are not equivalent across grade levels, creating conceptual inconsistency concerning the outcome measure.

Fortunately, because we did not compare the predictability of the instrument across grade levels but aggregated proportions together across grade levels, we do not expect the conceptual inconsistency to create any serious bias concerning the instrument. But, this issue requires some caution when researchers use the instrument to compare the effects of school leadership on student achievement across educational levels (e.g., between elementary school and middle school or across grade levels within elementary or middle school). In sum, the predictability of the instrument on student achievement (at the school level) may be grade-level specific (because of standard setting) and may lack direct comparability across grade levels. The application of the instrument to explore the effects of school leadership on student achievement aggregated across grade levels within a school is more appropriate and can be substantially effective.

In summary, the research in this chapter presents a framework of seven dimensions along which the principal and teachers could work together. There are many areas in which the principal and teachers could work together. The seven dimensions in this learning-centered leadership framework are just a beginning. To continue to develop areas in which the principal and teachers could work together will point to the "content" areas in which the principal and teachers could bridge the fault line.

APPENDIX 4.1: TEACHER SURVEY ON LEARNING-CENTERED SCHOOL LEADERSHIP

Directions to teachers: Please indicate your selection for each statement by using

1 = strongly disagree
2 = moderately disagree
3 = slightly disagree
4 = slightly agree

5 = moderately agree

6 = strongly agree

Data-informed decision-making

1 We consistently analyze student achievement to establish school improvement goals.

2 We collaborate with each other across grade levels to conduct inquiry using schoolwide data.

3 We have received adequate professional development on analyzing and interpreting data.

4 We have strong support from the central office administration for using data for decision-making.

5 We have sufficient technology to utilize the data we need.

6 We consistently use data from multiple sources to monitor student learning.

Safe and orderly school operation

7 We have comprehensive safety policies and procedures in place.

8 We have a positive school climate conducive to student learning.

9 We have good policies to protect students from cyber and other bullying.

10 We consistently monitor and work to reduce student behavior referrals.

11 Our building overall is in good physical condition.

12 We have policies that effectively promote respect for differences in our school environment.

High, cohesive, and culturally relevant expectations for all students

13 We have an effective process for students to set learning expectations for themselves.

14 Our teachers design learning activities that are relevant to our students' personal backgrounds.

15 We consistently share specific learning goals with our students.

16 Our school activities engage students and their families in ways that relate to their family circumstances and cultures.

17 We regularly monitor and address student achievement gaps.

18 We utilize strategies to engage parents fully as instructional partners.

Distributive and empowering leadership

19 The majority of our teachers are involved in school leadership activities via committees or other organizational structures.

20 We have an environment in which teachers feel very comfortable in offering input on needed improvements.

21 The majority of our teachers engage in peer observations and feedback.

22 We have an environment in which teachers work together closely on school improvement activities.

(cont.)

23 We have one or more fairly strong professional learning communities in place within our school.

24 We have a culture of collective responsibility among all teachers and staff within our school.

Coherent curricular programs

25 Our curriculum is well aligned horizontally and vertically across grades in our school.

26 Our teachers regularly meet to discuss how they are interpreting the curriculum and building lessons/units.

27 Our teachers regularly meet to share and evaluate instructional strategies for teaching the curriculum units and lessons.

28 Our teachers consistently meet to design student work and formative assessments.

29 Our teachers consistently communicate the key curriculum performance standards to students and parents.

30 Our students consistently track their own progress in mastering key curriculum performance standards.

Real-time and embedded instructional assessment

31 We consistently implement biweekly or more frequent assessments in each subject at each grade level.

32 Our teachers consistently use data from formative assessments to inform further instruction.

33 Our teachers meet with students on a regular basis to review their formative assessment data.

34 All our teachers understand and utilize formative assessments.

35 We consistently use different feedback strategies depending on the needs of the students.

36 Our students understand what they are to learn on a daily basis.

Commitment and passion for school renewal

37 We have a culture in which teachers hold themselves accountable for student achievement.

38 We have a school culture where teachers learn from each other.

39 We regularly celebrate our successes.

40 All of our teachers and staff are continuously seeking ways to enhance the teaching and learning processes in our school.

41 We have a clear, shared vision about what we want and expect for all students.

42 We have a positive school environment in which student learning is the primary focus.

APPENDIX 4.2: THE ONE- AND SEVEN-FACTOR MODELS

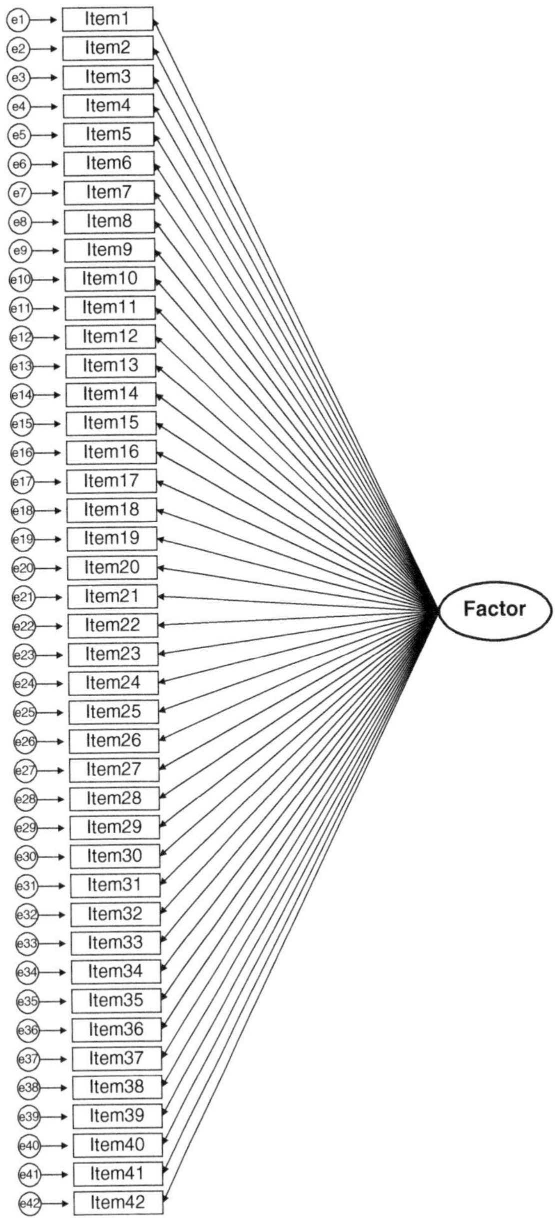

A.4.2.1 The one-factor model

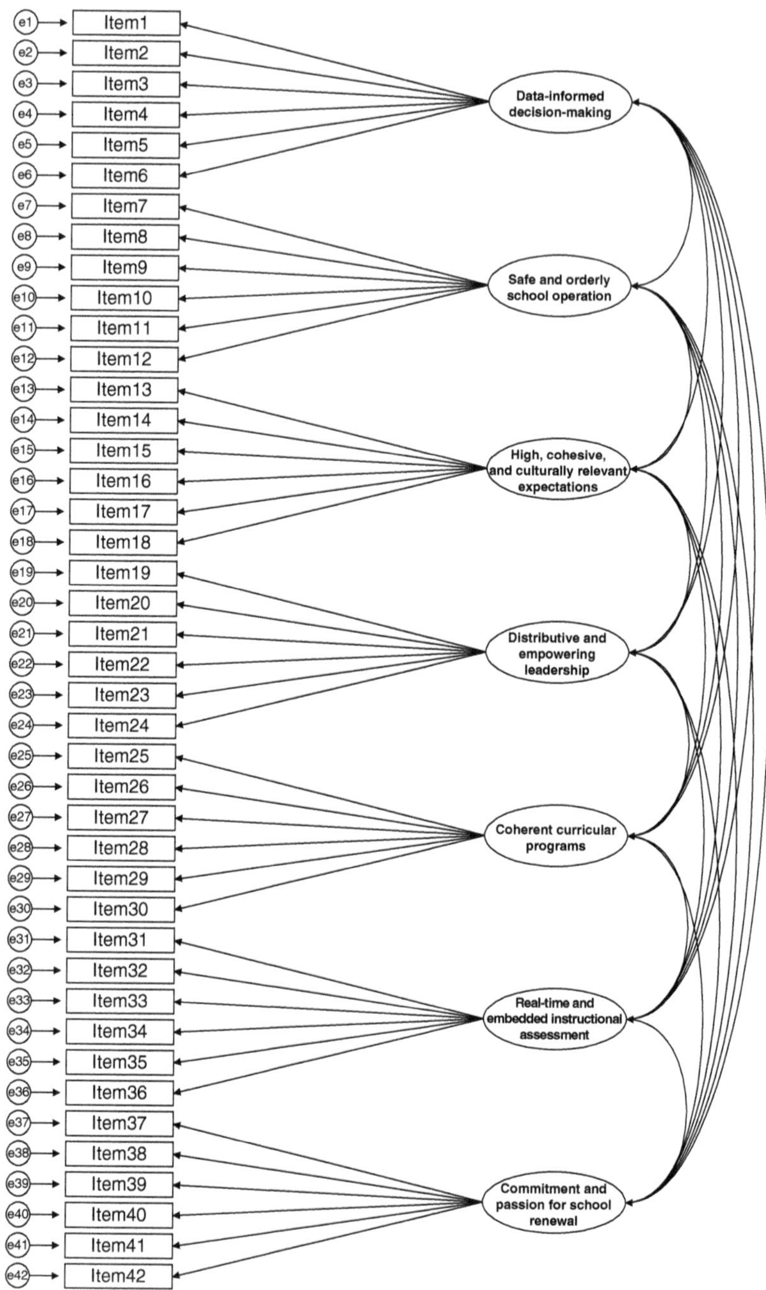

A.4.2.2 The seven-factor model

APPENDIX 4.3: DESCRIPTIVE STATISTICS OF DEPENDENT, CONTEXTUAL, AND PREDICTIVE VARIABLES

	Min	Max	Mean	SD
Dependent variables				
Mathematics (percentage of students at proficient level)	.00	79.00	19.53	17.22
Reading (percentage of students at proficient level)	.00	92.70	29.52	19.07
Contextual variables				
School enrollment (number of students)	14.00	779.00	225.00	151.38
Proportion of male students	.45	.93	.53	.07
Proportion of White students	.01	.97	.41	.32
Proportion of students eligible for free or reduced price lunch	.20	.96	.70	.17
Predictive variables				
Data-informed decision-making	3.05	5.67	4.38	.60
Safe and orderly school operation	2.58	6.00	4.35	.68
High, cohesive, and culturally relevant expectations for all students	3.01	6.00	4.32	.56
Distributive and empowering leadership	2.72	5.50	4.15	.63
Coherent curricular programs	2.00	5.33	3.91	.76
Real-time and embedded instructional assessment	3.13	5.33	4.23	.56
Commitment and passion for school renewal	3.00	5.50	4.50	.61
Total	2.91	5.48	4.26	.54

Note: Predictive variables come from the instrument with six components measured on a scale of 1–6, with a high value indicating a more positive response.

CHAPTER 5

Orientation to School Renewal

A Framework of "Process" for School Renewal

INTRODUCTION

How to improve our schools is a challenge to policymakers, school personnel, and the general public. Improvement efforts often focus on developing content-based programs such as a mathematics curriculum, a reading program, or an after-school program. Few efforts have focused on the process of improving our schools, and when they do, a reform model approach is often used, with an emphasis on top-down, implementation fidelity and accountability measures (Reeves et al., 2014; Shen, 2015; Shen & Cooley, 2015). Given this, our team's school improvement efforts and research have been advocating for a process called "school renewal" (rather than school reform). Table 5.1 reveals the major dimensions of our school renewal model, in contrast to the more traditional school reform approach (Shen, 2020; Shen & Burt, 2015).

The school renewal model is based on the body of literature on school renewal (e.g., Goodlad, 1975a, 1975b; Soder, 1999; Sirotnik, 1999), grant-supported improvement efforts, reflections with school principals and teachers, and our research (Reeves et al., 2014; Shen, 2015; Shen & Cooley, 2013, 2015). The elements of the school renewal concept, the implementation and manifestation of the renewal concept in action, and effects of the renewal approach have been explained in an edited book by Shen and Burt (2015). In this chapter, we demonstrate the factorial validity, reliability, and predictive validity for student achievement. Corresponding to the conceptualization of the differences between the school reform and renewal model, the Orientation for School Renewal instrument entails seven dimensions of school renewal efforts: (a) focus on students and their achievement; (b) continuous school improvement;

Table 5.1 *School reform model versus school renewal model*

The "reform" model	The "renewal" model
Shifting focus	Focus on students and their achievement (F1)
Driven by the reform agenda	Continuous school improvement (F2)
Externally driven	Balance between the internal and external influences (F3)
The research, development, dissemination and evaluation (RDDE) model	The dialogue, decision, action, and evaluation (DDAE) model (F4)
Implementation fidelity	Implementation integrity (F5)
Implementers as passive receivers	Implementers as active developers (F6)
External accountability	Internal responsibility and professionalism (F7)

(c) balance between the internal and external influences; (d) the dialogue, decision, action, and evaluation (DDAE) model (Goodlad, 1975a, 1975b); (e) implementation integrity; (f) implementers as active developers; and (g) internal responsibility and professionalism. In the following, we provide a context for the instrument by reviewing the literature on the school reform and school renewal, and on the seven dimensions of school renewal.

THE CHALLENGE IN FINDING AN EFFECTIVE STRATEGY TO SCHOOL IMPROVEMENT

Multiple organizations, politicians, the media, and educational leaders continue to call for the transformation of the American public educational system. Starting with the 1983 A Nation at Risk Report, and continuing with the Every Student Succeeds Act, billions of dollars have been poured into the US public educational system. In response, many educational change efforts have been implemented, and much has been learned. Yet, some fundamental questions remain unanswered. What should be the roles of principals and teachers in helping make changes to achieve higher outcomes for all students? Are they merely faithful implementers? Should changes be wholesale or incremental?

Should change be driven and shaped by highly prescribed policy frames for school improvement? A common thread in the earlier questions is the overall approach to school improvement. In this chapter, we investigate the construct of "school renewal," as opposed to "school reform." School reform is often more top-down, with a focus on accountability measures (e.g., Shen & Cooley, 2015; Shen, 2020), compared to a more organic approach with educators determining how best to "renew" their organizations.

In this chapter, we use "school improvement" as a neutral term to refer to the efforts to better our schools. Within the school improvement efforts, we distinguish between "school reform" and "school renewal." School reform is top-down and externally driven with a focus on external accountability while "school renewal" reflects the creative tension between the internal and external forces, with a focus on internal responsibility and professionalism. Our construct of school renewal coincides with current theories of teacher leadership, which view leadership as a process operating in an organization, rather than a process operated by an individual (Muijs & Harris, 2006). Yet, a subtle nuance is that while teacher leadership theories tend to focus on the aspects of shared responsibility and teacher empowerment, our construct of school renewal focuses on the aspect of constructing a more balanced and sustainable school ecosystem, thereby places a greater emphasis on the interconnections within the school community.

Just as medical researchers know that many multi-factor diseases have no single cure, educational researchers, school leaders, and classroom teachers are also discovering that different strategies work better in different educational communities and schools (Wu et al., 2020). Even when school change efforts center on well validated, research-supported initiatives, systemic issues such as implementation integrity, fidelity, and sustainability are requiring ongoing attention to key school conditions that determine the school's capacity for adaptive change (Fixsen et al., 2005).

Systemic issues, by their natures, need to be solved with a systemic approach. To achieve broader and deeper changes in organizations, leadership is more and more about pulling people's ideas and information together than simply bringing people together. Therefore, the improvement agenda and corresponding strategies could be translated into real-world practice by each person within the system. Sergiovanni (2005) pointed out that, leadership was a group activity linked to practice rather than just an individual activity linked to a person. Indeed, researchers have noted that purveyors (e.g., school personnel) for change must play an essential role in implementing school renewal efforts including exploration and adoption, program installation, full operation, innovation, and sustainability (Fixsen et al., 2010). School personnel are, therefore, not mere implementers, but they must be engaged in the development of such efforts as well. Silva et al. (2002) differentiated three types of teacher leadership roles. The first one was the most common – the head teacher role, whose job was to improve the school efficiency like a traditional "manager." The second role was a curriculum expert or an instructional leader, as teachers could establish leadership in their professional daily work. The third role, however, was the re-designers (educational innovators) or agents (cultural changers). For this role, teachers influence those more fundamental elements of school organizations, including the "goals, structure, roles, and norms of an organization" (p. 781).

THE ROLE OF SCHOOL PERSONNEL IN SCHOOL IMPROVEMENT

Although findings may vary (Bowers, 2020; Berkovich, 2016; Jacob et al., 2015), there appears to be some agreement that school principals and teachers are pivotal actors in student learning and school improvement (Hallinger & Heck, 2010b; Liebowitz & Porter, 2019; Pont et al., 2008; Wu et al., 2019). For example, a few recent meta-analyses (Tan et al., 2020; Shen & Wu, 2024; Wu & Shen, 2022) found positive overall relationships between principal leadership, on the one hand, and student, teacher, and organizational outcomes, on the other. Their synthesis also revealed that principals impact student outcomes through a wide range of practices and some practices may be more effective than others. In the most recent Wallace Foundation synthesis report, Grissom et al. (2021) summarized evidence from six rigorous studies using longitudinal design to examine principals' effect, a synthesis that helps to better understand the causal relationship between principal leadership and student outcomes than correlational studies.

Their results showed that effective principals have a large effect on a range of outcomes, and the importance of principals may have even been underestimated previously. Likewise, studies have also revealed that teacher leadership is positively associated with student and school outcomes (Sebastian et al., 2016; Shen et al., 2020; Rhodes et al., 2009; Wu et al., 2020).

Despite the foci on the effectiveness of either principal leadership or teacher leadership, a limited number of studies assessed leadership impact as a function of combined efforts by both school principals and teachers. As Hallinger and Heck (2010b) have suggested, to fully capture the school leadership effect, researchers need to take into account the reciprocal-effect between principal leadership and teacher leadership. Shen (2020) argued that the educational system in the US is bifurcated (rather than loosely coupled), with a fault line between the state-district-school tectonic plate and the classroom tectonic plate. Therefore, to effectively bridge this fault line is a challenge for efforts on educational improvement. He advocated the construct of "school leadership" by integrating principal leadership and teacher leaders to focus on those school leadership dimensions in which both the principal and teachers could engage.

A literature review by Daniëls et al. (2019) summarized key areas of effective school leadership: a focus on curricula and instruction; strong communication and good internal and external relations; shaping the organizational climate and culture, including trust and collaboration; defining and sustaining a school's vision and mission; providing frequent feedback and recognizing acknowledgments; and hiring and retaining qualified teachers and investing in their professional development. This list is similar to a unified framework created by Hitt and Tucker (2016) in which effective school leaders must facilitate a high-quality learning experience; establish and convey the vision; build professional capacity; create a supportive organization for learning; and connect with external partners. School leaders now have access to a plethora of lists from which they can draw to shape their day-to-day practices. Some provide frameworks or developmental rubrics and even finely calibrated scales (Carbaugh et al., 2015) that explicitly identify high impact behaviors and actions. Moreover, as states adopted new statutes requiring robust teacher and administrator evaluation systems in response to federal policy requirements, these tools have begun to replace outdated and poorly developed educator evaluation instruments and systems (Michigan Council for Educator Effectiveness, 2013). The assumption is that providing better measures of teacher and principal performance characteristics will lead to more effective teachers and school leaders.

Yet, having a repertoire of leadership and instructional practices is not enough; principals and teacher leaders need situational awareness and contextual understanding to inform where, how, and when to employ specific leadership and instructional practices, and a systemic approach to put those practices to work. To achieve such situational and contextual understanding of their schools, they must draw upon evidence-based and data-informed processes (Shen & Burt, 2015). However, while the importance of school leaders as purveyors of change, and in establishing school processes, routines, and systems that support such change is well established, there are still few models for developing principals' and teacher leaders' capacity to do so (Shaked & Schechter, 2016). Many school leaders and teacher teams are still limited in their capacity to establish evidence-based and data-informed processes in their schools for the lack of a systemic approach.

This gets to the crux of the problem. Principals and teacher leaders need systemic models for how to prioritize, map, align, monitor, and adapt a pathway that best fits their school to achieve implementation integrity for high-impact strategies needed to improve student success (Shen & Cooley, 2012, 2015). This chapter delves into the "renewal" model.

EFFORTS TO REFINE AN IMPROVEMENT STRATEGY: SCHOOL RENEWAL

The late eminent educational scholar, John Goodlad, was the first to propose the idea of renewal in the 1970s. At that time, he dichotomized the constructs of "school reform" and "school renewal." He criticized the "research, development, dissemination, and evaluation" (RDDE) model in school reform, and advocated the "dialogue, decision, action, and evaluation" (DDAE) model as an approach to school renewal (Goodlad, 1975a, 1975b, 1999; Shen, 1999).

On the difference between school reform and school renewal, Soder (1999), one of Goodlad's colleagues, said that "embedded in both 'reform' and 'renewal' are basic views of the world, basic views of human nature, and basic views of the ways we do business in this world" (p. 568). Soder differentiated reform from renewal: "you can tell people what to do [reform], or you can let people determine their purposes and ways to achieve them [renewal]" (p. 568). Michelli (2016), the first chair of the National Network for Educational Renewal, noted that "Reform is negative, pejorative, and finite. Renewal is positive and ongoing" (p. 149). The aim of our work was to develop an instrument that measures school renewal, as described in this article.

SCHOOL REFORM AND SCHOOL RENEWAL IN AN INTERNATIONAL CONTEXT

School reform and school renewal have been prominent international topics in the field of education (Harris & Hopkins, 1999). For example, in the US, scholars have distinguished the "reform" and "renewal" model and advocated the notion of "renewal" (Goodlad, 1975a, 1975b; Joyce & Calhoun, 1995; Joyce et al., 1993; Sirotnik, 1999; Soder, 1999). In the United Kingdom, school "reform versus renewal" has been a debated topic (Egan & Marshall, 2007; Hopkins, 2013; Hopkins et al., 1997). The "Improving the Quality of Education for All (IQEA)" project is a model that reflects the idea of school renewal. It aims to build the school capacity for cultural change. Furthermore, researchers in the UK have also attempted to develop multilevel intervention (at the classroom and school level) for sustaining school improvement (Harris & Hopkins, 1999, 2000; Harris & Young, 2000). In other European countries, educational reform/renewal attempts in various countries, including Finland (Sahlberg, 2011), Netherland (Sleegers & Wesselingh, 1995), Sweden (Lundahl et al., 2010), and central and eastern Europe (Cerych, 1997), have been documented and widely discussed.

SEVEN DIMENSIONS OF SCHOOL RENEWAL

Based on the literature and our projects in the field, the following seven dimensions were distilled to reflect the construct of school renewal.

Dimension 1 of School Renewal: Focus on Students and Their Achievement

Improving student achievement is the focus of all schools and some are more successful than others. For example, Lezotte's (1991) seminal study synthesized seven correlates of effective schools and all these correlates focus on students and their achievement. Later on, Gunal and Demirtasli (2016) demonstrated that a focus on students and their achievement is associated with better student outcomes. Marzano et al. (2005), Osborne-Lampkin et al. (2015), and Barr (2016) found that school climate with a focus on students and their achievement was a critical element in improving student outcomes. Multiple student-centered programs have also been shown to bring great benefit to students and schools. This is depicted in studies conducted by Nunnery et al. (2011), who reported a statistically significant effect on both students' math and ELA performance at elementary and middle school levels, as the intervention group outperformed the control group with an effect size (in Cohen's d) of 0.14 in math, and 0.11 in English language arts.

Dimension 2 of School Renewal: Continuous School Improvement

Continuous school improvement is one important dimension that differentiates school renewal from school reform. Joyce and Calhoun (1995) argued that school renewal is not a formula, but an inquiry. It inquiries into recreating school organizations through changes that "support continuous examination and improvement of the education process at every level (Joyce & Calhoun 1995, p. 51)." Similarly, Sirotnik (1999) noted that compared to school reform, school renewal is "not about a point in time; it is about all points in time – it is about continuous, critical inquiry into current practices and principled innovation that might improve education (pp. 607–608)." In both business and education, continuous improvement is a popular construct (Aguayo, 1990; Garvin, 1993; Garvin et al., 2008; Y. L. Goddard et al., 2007; Hitt, 1995; Senge, 1990; Senge et al., 2012, 2007; Starratt, 1996; Yukl, 1989). Based on the traditional, four-step Continuous Improvement Model developed by Deming

(1986) – plan-do-check/study-act/adjust, Bernhardt (2004) proposed a plan-implement-evaluate-improve strategy for continuous school improvement. The characteristic of continuous improvement teams is their ability to engage members in the process of dialogue where there is honest and open communication (Bernhardt, 2004; Hitt, 1995; Senge et al., 2012) and collaboration between staff members (Hitt, 1995; Kline & Saunders, 1998; Woodland et al., 2013). Empirical studies indicate that the continuous improvement process has positive effects on student outcome measures (e.g., Bitter et al., 2009). A study even estimated the size of the effect of continuous improvement on student achievement to be greater than 0.80 in terms of Cohen's d (Gallimore et al., 2009).

Dimension 3 of School Renewal: Balance between the Internal and External Influences

In the 1970s researchers such as Berman and McLaughlin (1976) described the policy implementation process as a process of mutual adaptation, meaning that the policy adapts to the context and the context adapts to the policy. During the past decades, American schools have witnessed increasing emphasis on holding schools accountable for student achievement (Hanushek & Raymond, 2005). As many researchers have noted, the strict accountability policy has deeply changed the dynamics of school work (Lee & Wong, 2004) and academic goals of schools (Shen et al., 2005). Therefore, one great challenge our school leaders today are facing is how to strike a balance between internal and external influences. Typically, internal influence refers to stakeholders inside of school, including the need of students and teachers; while external influence comes from stakeholders outside of schools, including pressure from Local Education Agencies (LEAs), parents, and policymakers. Although a school's external and internal stakeholders tend to have different agendas (Honig & Hatch, 2004; Thornton & Perreault, 2002) and mental models (Datnow & Hubbard, 2015; Jimerson & McGhee, 2013), it is possible to balance the internal and external influences. Existing research has suggested the following: (a) we must engage schools in the endogenous dynamics of forming learning organizations where the practitioners have "shared understanding and commitment to achieve high level outcomes for all students" (Fullan, 2007, p. 5); (b) an individual teacher or teacher communities must understand, adapt, and re-shape external policies into local environment (e.g., Spillane, 1999); and (c) schools need to actively and closely cooperate with districts while districts act as a mediator between state policy and school practice (Honig & Hatch, 2004; Spillane, 1994, 1998, 1999).

Dimension 4 of School Renewal: The Dialogue, Decision, Action, and Evaluation (DDAE) Model

A synthesis of the current empirical research encourages the use of dialogue, discussion, action, and evaluation to support the improvement of teaching and student learning (Bitter et al., 2009; Black & Wiliam, 1998; Carlson et al., 2011; Campbell & Levin, 2009; Lai & McNaughton, 2016; Marsh et al., 2015; Schildkamp & Poortman, 2015; Shin et al., 2004; Van Geel et al., 2016). Empirical studies (Bitter et al., 2009; Darling-Hammond et al., 2002), including some that involved randomized selection (e.g., Carlson et al., 2011; Slavin et al., 2013), found positive effects of elements of the DDAE process on student outcomes.

Dimension 5 of School Renewal: Implementation Integrity

Researchers have studied the school improvement process with multiple frames or assumptions. Two divergent schools of thought are implementation fidelity and integrity. In the literature, implementation fidelity means that the implementation follows the intended model (Century & Cassata, 2016). Ideas around implementation fidelity assume there is one correct way to implement an innovation, and that implementation is a linear and rational process (Hulleman & Cordray, 2009; Smith et al., 2013; Strain & Bovey, 2011). Another perspective is implementation integrity, which means the improvement process plays out in context. This school of thought assumes that school improvement cannot, and indeed perhaps should not, play out strictly in a model way. Studies by Barab and Luehmann (2003), Fogleman et al. (2011), Forbes and Davis (2010) examined the integrity of the implementation, or the adaptation of the innovation to the context. In practice, it has been noted that an educational program cannot produce an intended benefit without being fully integrated into the school's everyday processes and actual practices

(Roberts-Gray et al., 2007). Empirical studies indicate that implementation integrity is feasible and effective (Roberts-Gray et al., 2007). Data play a significant role in implementation integrity (Bernhardt, 2009; Datnow & Hubbard, 2015; Gunter & Fitzgerald, 2013).

Dimension 6 of School Renewal: Implementers as Active Developers

Previous research has revealed that school leadership tends to affect student achievement indirectly through intervening variables such as organizational capacity, teacher commitment, and cooperation (Heck & Hallinger, 2014; Leithwood et al., 2010; Scheerens, 2012). Researchers have been identifying specific intervening variables with positive connections to student achievement outcomes, such as organizational citizenship behaviors and school-level collective efficacy. Organizational citizenship describes the additional efforts teachers put forth outside their classrooms to support school goals and school-level collective efficacy describes the shared experiences and beliefs of the teachers about the collective agency of their school to meet goals. Numerous studies have demonstrated that school-level collective efficacy has positive, independent effects on student achievement (e.g., Leithwood & Jantzi, 2008; Robinson, et al., 2008), even when controlling for the effects of low student socioeconomic status (e.g., Boberg & Bourgeois, 2016; Moolenaar et al., 2012), as does the additional effort teachers put forward as part of organizational citizen behaviors (e.g., Zeinabadi, 2014). Research efforts continue with the goal of better understanding the specific school-level actions and behaviors that lead to improved student achievement outcomes. These include variables examined in our school renewal instrument such as teachers and their principal being active developers of the instructional strategies and programs they are implementing (i.e., a type of organizational citizen behavior).

Dimension 7 of School Renewal: Internal Responsibility and Professionalism

Sergiovanni (2005) and Harris (2005) noted that teachers assume more internal responsibilities at both the instructional and organizational levels. By accepting and actively practicing their internal responsibility and professionalism, teachers become more self-motivated, committed to learning, and satisfied (Fullan, 2007; Senge, 1990), accountable to themselves (Dufour, 2004), and gradually assume the roles of leaders and initiators for improvement (Phillips, 2003; Senge, 1990), learners and learning facilitators (Stoll et al., 2006), and collaborators (Firestone, 2009; Louis, 2006). A series of studies by Hallinger and Heck (1996a, 1996b, 1998, 2010a, 2010b) highlighted the interaction between school leaders and the sense of responsibility and professionalism in their schools. Garet et al. (2010) reported a randomized controlled study where a professional development program on teachers' internal responsibility and professionalism had a statistically significant impact on teachers' frequency of engaging in activities that elicited student thinking, with an effect size of 0.48, an effect size measure that is similar to Cohen's *d* based on mean difference between the treatment and control groups divided by control group's standard deviation, with the mean difference derived from the multilevel level modeling estimation.

DEVELOPING AND VALIDATING THE SEVEN-FACTOR SCHOOL RENEWAL FRAMEWORK

The earlier sections of this chapter outline the challenges in school improvement, the difference between school reform and school renewal, and the seven dimensions of school renewal based on literature review and working with schools on funded projects. In this section, results for validating the Orientation to School Renewal – including the factorial validity of the construct of school renewal, reliability, and the instrument's predictive validity for school-level achievement – are presented and discussed.

Developing the Instrument "Orientation for School Renewal"

We developed the Orientation to School Renewal instrument with a goal of making it both effective (sensitive) and efficient (concise) for practical applications by both researchers and practitioners. The process followed the five-step procedure for instrument validation established in the classic paper by Clark and Watson (1995), including (a) analysis of item distribution; (b) unidimensionality, internal consistency, and coefficient alpha; (c) the "attenuation paradox"; (d) structural analyses in scale construction; and (e) creating subscales. Applying these steps to our instrument development, we first conducted a number of comprehensive reviews of the research literature pertaining to how school renewal is understood, in association with three federally funded projects with a common theme of developing principal and teacher leadership with an emphasis on school renewal (in contrast to school reform) over the course of about five years for each of the grants. Researchers and practitioners engaged in a constant discussion on what school renewal means, and the major features of the construct. A table gradually took shape in an iterative manner that contrasts the constructs of school renewal and school reform, and reflects both the literature and our experiences (see Table 5.1). Second, based on this table, we developed indicators that address various aspects of school renewal (i.e., the proposed factors). In total, we constructed seven factors (F1 = Focus on students and their achievement; F2 = Continuous school improvement; F3 = Balance between the internal and external influences; F4 = The dialogue, decision, action, and evaluation (DDAE) process; F5 = Implementation integrity; F6 = Implementers as active developers; and F7 = Internal responsibility and professionalism). Third, we constructed items that operationalize each factor. In total, we developed twenty-one items with three measuring each factor (see Appendix 5.1). Each item came with a six-point (Likert-type) response scale ranging from "strongly disagree" to "strongly agree" with, when coded, a higher value indicating a more positive response. Fourth, we used a panel of experts to ensure the construct validity of the instrument. This panel consisted of experienced academic scholars and school leaders. Items were revised based on the feedback of the panel. Finally, we piloted the instrument with volunteer teachers in eighty-three schools. After a good result on the construct validity, we moved on to examine the structure and behavior of the instrument through a number of statistical procedures.

Data Sources

During the course of about eight years (2011–2018), our research team at Western Michigan University engaged in three federally funded projects (Learning-Centered Leadership Development Program,

Achievement-Centered Leadership Development Program, and Developing a Leadership Pipeline and Turning Around Schools Simultaneously). To conduct research related to our instrument, we combined participants from the three federally funded projects. As a result, we obtained responses on school renewal efforts from 1,195 school teachers who were on an instructional contract with a school and spent at least half of their teaching time in that school. These school teachers came from eighty-three schools, among which thirty-four were elementary schools, fifteen were a combination of elementary and middle school grades, nine were middle schools, ten were a combination of middle and high school grades, and fifteen were high schools. Data on school academic performance and school contextual characteristics were obtained from a public source for these schools. We collected information on critical school contextual characteristics, including percentage of male students (a measure of school gender composition), percentage of White students (a measure of school racial–ethnic composition), and percentage of students eligible for free lunch (a measure of school socioeconomic composition). The key outcome measure or dependent variable were school academic performance in our study using two academic performance measures. The school academic performance outcome came from the Michigan Student Test of Educational Progress (M-STEP) for students in Grades 3–8 in mathematics and English language arts (ELA).

Findings on the Factorial Validity and Reliability of the Instrument "Orientation to School Renewal"

One key step in operationalizing the construct of "school renewal" is to investigate its factorial validity. In other words, factorial validity examines, among other things, how the items measure a factor and how the factors are related to each other. Factorial validity, a type of construct validity, studies how the underlying structure of an instrument (the seven dimensions of the construct of "school renewal" in this case), as measured by a factor analysis, reflects the intended construct.

As to the factorial validity, we conducted confirmatory factor analysis (CFA) and tested three models. The first CFA tested a one-factor model with all of the items loaded on one common factor (i.e., a single factor

Table 5.2 *Model-data-fit indices for testing factorial validity*

Model	χ^2	CFI	TLI	SRMR	RMSEA
Null model	23193.53	–	–	–	–
One factor model	4274.80	0.822	0.805	0.228	0.134
Seven factor model	1763.57	0.931	0.913	0.037	0.089
Higher-order factor model	2165.28	0.914	0.900	0.040	0.095

Note: CFI = comparative fit index; TLI = Tucker-Lewis index; SRMR = standardized root mean square residual; and RMSEA = root mean square error of approximation.

of "school renewal"). The second CFA tested the seven-factor model that we derived from the literature (i.e., the school renewal framework in Table 5.1). The third CFA tested a second-order factor structure in which the seven factors (from the second model) also loaded on one higher-order mega factor given that they all addressed the latent construct of school renewal. Please see Appendix 5.2 for details on the measurement models. As usual, the null model served as the baseline model for all comparisons.

Following the common statistical practices, we used various fitting indices in this validation process to assess and compare the results of the CFAs. Specifically, they were chi-square, comparative fit index (CFI) (Bentler, 1990), Tucker-Lewis index (TLI) (Bentler & Bonett, 1980), as well as standardized root mean square residual (SRMR) and root mean square error of approximation (RMSEA) (Hu & Bentler, 1999). We adopted the established guidelines to use (at least) .90 as the cutoff value for both CFI and TLI and (at most) .08 as the cutoff value for both SRMR and RMSEA.

The findings in Table 5.2 indicate that the seven-factor model fits the data the best: .931 for CFI, .913 for TLI, .037 for SRMR, and .089 for RMSEA. These fitting indices for the seven-factor structure either came close to (in the case of RMSEA) or surpassed the corresponding established cutoff values (in the cases of CFI, TLI, and SRMR), indicating acceptable model-data-fit results for the seven-factor model.

The comparison between the seven factors model and the higher-order factor model also indicated the superiority of the seven-factor model across all model-data-fit indices (1763.57 vs 2165.28 on χ^2, .931

Table 5.3 *Internal consistency (Cronbach's alpha) for subscales and overall scale*

Factor	α
F1. Focus on students and their achievement	.835
F2. Continuous school improvement	.807
F3. Balance between the internal and external influences	.898
F4. The dialogue, decision, action, and evaluation process	.890
F5. Implementation integrity	.923
F6. Implementers as active developers	.829
F7. Internal responsibility and professionalism	.860
Whole Instrument	.974

vs .914 on CFI, .913 vs .900 on TLI, .037 vs .040 on SRMR, .089 vs .095 on RMSEA). Even if one were to argue that the model-data-fit results were roughly comparable between the two models, the simpler structure of the seven factors model would still be clearly preferable as a more efficient model for practical applications. Overall, the model-data-fit results confirmed from multiple perspectives that the original specification of the twenty-one items on the seven factors was strongly supported by the data. Therefore, it is valid to conceptualize the construct of "school renewal" along the seven dimensions.

We also found, in Table 5.3, very strong internal consistencies (Cronbach's alpha), one commonly used form of reliability, across the seven factors (from .807 to .923) and for the whole instrument (.974). Based on the general guideline of (at least) .80 as the cutoff value for α (Nunnally & Bernstein, 1994), all of these reliability measures surpassed the cutoff value for Cronbach's alpha as we discussed earlier. Please refer to Shen et al. (2021) for other psychometric analyses for factor loading, R^2, and discrimination index (D) among the items.

Findings on Effects of School Renewal on M-STEP

Table 5.4 presents multiple regression results on the relationship between school academic performance on M-STEP and school renewal efforts. Because school contextual characteristics were used as control variables, Table 5.4 (and also upcoming Table 5.5) omitted their results

Table 5.4 *Instrument predicting school performance (within-school percentage of students at proficient and advanced levels)*

Factor	Mathematics			ELA		
	Effect	SE	R^2	Effect	SE	R^2
D1. Focus on students and their achievement	9.96*	2.34	.29	3.84*	1.85	.45
D2. Continuous school improvement	7.42*	2.35	.26	3.67*	1.82	.45
D3. Balance between the internal and external influences	6.48*	2.02	.26	2.63	1.52	.45
D4. The dialogue, decision, action, and evaluation (DDAE) model	5.39*	1.75	.26	2.54[†]	1.37	.45
D5. Implementation integrity	5.04*	1.85	.25	3.38*	1.44	.46
D6. Implementers as active developers	6.39*	2.01	.26	4.01*	1.57	.46
D7. Internal responsibility	8.10*	1.93	.29	5.53*	1.49	.48
Overall	7.93*	2.16	.27	4.26*	1.69	.46

Note: Mathematics and ELA are analyzed separately as school performance outcomes. For each school performance outcome, dimensions (and overall) are analyzed separately in the presence of all control variables of school characteristics. Effect = unstandardized regression coefficient. SE = standard error. R^2 = proportion of variance in each school performance outcome explained by a multiple regression model. The outcome measure is the current year school-level M-STEP proficiency rate (at the proficient or advanced level), with a mean of 21.96 and standard deviation of 16.12 for mathematics, and 29.82 and 15.68 for ELA. *$p < .05$. [†]$p < .07$.

for a focus on the key variables of school renewal efforts as predictors. For mathematics, each and every factor as well as the whole measure of school renewal efforts were statistically significant at the standard alpha level of .05 with all of the effects in the positive direction. For example, a one-unit increase (on the measurement scale of 1–6) in the effort to focus on students and their achievement was associated with a nearly ten-percentage-point increase in terms of the proportion of students who reached the proficient and advanced categories in mathematics at the grade level. Putting all school renewal efforts together (i.e., the whole instrument), a one-unit increase (on the measurement scale of 1–6) in school renewal efforts was associated with a nearly eight-percentage-point increase in terms of the proportion of students who reached the proficient and advanced categories in mathematics at the grade level. In a comparative sense, Dimension 1 (Focus on students and their achievement), Dimension 7 (Internal responsibility), and Dimension 2 (Continuous school improvement) were the leading dimensions of school renewal efforts that were most strongly related to school academic performance in M-STEP mathematics (effect = 9.96, 8.10, and 7.42, respectively).

For ELA five out of the seven dimensions as well as the whole measure of school renewal efforts were statistically significant at the standard alpha level of .05, and one out of the remaining two dimensions was statistically significant marginally (at the alpha level of .07). All of the effects were in the right direction (i.e., positive). For example, a one-unit increase (on the measurement scale of 1–6) in the effort to focus on students and their achievement was associated with a nearly four-percentage-point increase in terms of the proportion of students who reached the proficient and advanced categories in ELA at the grade level. Putting all school renewal efforts together (i.e., the whole instrument), a one-unit increase (on the measurement scale of 1–6) in school renewal efforts was associated with a nearly six-percentage-point increase in terms of the proportion of students who reached the proficient and advanced categories in ELA at the grade level. Only one dimension was not statistically significant, Dimension 3 (Balance between the internal and external influences). In a comparative sense, Dimension 7 (Internal responsibility and professionalism) stood out from the group as the clearly leading dimension of school renewal efforts that was most strongly related to school academic performance in M-STEP language (effect = 5.53).

Considering all data together, we concluded that school renewal efforts tended to demonstrate a clearly stronger association with school academic performance in mathematics than school academic performance in language. The pattern was very evident, with each and every dimension showing a stronger association with school academic performance in mathematics than school academic performance in ELA. The whole measure of school renewal efforts followed the same pattern as well.

Finally, the R^2 provided us with a way to assess the performance of our multiple regression models. We found that the multiple regression model explained between 25 percent and 29 percent of the variance in the proportion of students who reached the proficient and advanced categories in mathematics at the grade level. Meanwhile, our multiple regression model explained between 45 percent and 48 percent of the variance in the proportion of students who reached the proficient and advanced categories in ELA at the grade level. These percentages were rather acceptable indications that the multiple regression models performed well in explaining the variance in the proportion of students who reached the proficient and advanced categories in both mathematics and language at the grade level.

Findings on Effects of School Renewal on Gains in M-STEP

The result in this section focused on "gains" in M-STEP. Prior year mathematics school-level proficiency level was entered as a control when the current year mathematics school-level proficiency level was used as an outcome measure. Prior year ELA proficiency level was used as a control variable when current year ELA school-level proficiency level was used as an outcome measure. All other variables were the same as those in the previous section. With control for prior year school-level proficiency rate, the regression coefficients represent "gains" in proficiency rate. Table 5.5 presents multiple regression results on the relationship between gains in school academic performance in M-STEP and school renewal efforts. For mathematics, almost all dimensions as well as the whole measure of school renewal efforts were statistically significant at the standard alpha level of .05 with all of the effects in the positive direction. For example, a one-unit increase (on the measurement scale of 1–6) in the effort to focus on students and their achievement was associated with a gain of nearly five-percentage-points in the proportion of students who reached the proficient and advanced categories in mathematics at the grade level from the previous year to the current year. Putting all school renewal efforts together (i.e., the whole instrument), a one-unit increase (on the measurement scale of 1–6) in school renewal efforts was associated with a gain of nearly four-percentage-points in the proportion of students who reached the proficient and advanced categories in mathematics at the grade level from the previous year to the current

Table 5.5 *Instrument predicting gains in school performance (within-school percentage of students at proficient and advanced levels)*

Factor	Mathematics			ELA		
	Effect	SE	R^2	Effect	SE	R^2
D1. Focus on students and their achievement	4.87*	1.78	.65	2.35	1.54	.63
D2. Continuous school improvement	4.13*	1.76	.65	1.82	1.55	.62
D3. Balance between the internal and external influences	4.52*	1.45	.66	2.26[†]	1.24	.63
D4. The dialogue, decision, action, and evaluation (DDAE) model	3.05*	1.26	.65	1.51	1.12	.62
D5. Implementation integrity	2.32	1.34	.65	2.26[†]	1.17	.63
D6. Implementers as active developers	3.12*	1.60	.65	2.25	1.43	.63
D7. Internal responsibility	3.60*	1.50	.65	3.67*	1.29	.64
Overall	4.23*	1.63	.65	2.74[†]	1.43	.63

Note: Mathematics and ELA are analyzed separately as school performance outcomes. For each school performance outcome, dimensions (and overall) are analyzed separately in the presence of all control variables of school characteristics and the prior year's school-level M-STEP proficiency rate. Effect = unstandardized regression coefficient. *SE* = standard error. R^2 = proportion of variance in each school performance outcome explained by a multiple regression model. The outcome measure is the current year school-level M-STEP proficiency rate (at the proficient or advanced level), with a mean of 21.96 and standard deviation of 16.12 for mathematics, and 29.82 and 15.68 for ELA. *$p < .05$. [†]$p < .07$

year. In a comparative sense, D1 (Focus on students and their achievement), D3 (Balance between the internal and external influences), and D2 (Continuous school improvement) were the leading dimensions of school renewal efforts that were most strongly related to gains in school academic performance in mathematics (effect = 4.87, 4.52, and 4.13, respectively).

For ELA, one dimension, D7 (Internal responsibility and Professionalism), was statistically significant at the standard alpha level of .05, and two out of the remaining six dimensions were statistically significant marginally (at the alpha level of .07), D3 (Balance between the internal and external influences) and D5 (Implementation integrity).

The whole measure of school renewal efforts was also marginally statistically significant (at the alpha level of .07). All of the statistically significant effects were in the positive direction. For example, a one-unit increase (on the measurement scale of 1–6) in internal responsibility was associated with a gain of nearly four-percentage-points in the proportion of students who reached the proficient and advanced categories in ELA at the grade level from the previous year to the current year. Putting all school renewal efforts together (i.e., the whole instrument), a one-unit increase (on the measurement scale of 1–6) in school renewal efforts was associated with a gain of nearly three-percentage-points in the proportion of students who reached the proficient and advanced categories in language at the grade level from the previous year to the current year. In a comparative sense, Dimension 7 (Internal responsibility) stood out from the group as the clearly leading dimension of school renewal efforts that was most strongly related to gains in school academic performance in language. Considering all the data together, the same pattern we discussed earlier occurred; that is, the school renewal efforts tended to demonstrate a clearly stronger association with gains in school academic performance in mathematics than gains in school academic performance in ELA.

Finally, the regression models accounted for 65 percent of the variance in gains in the proportion of students who reached the proficient and advanced categories in mathematics at the grade level and between 62 percent and 64 percent of the variance in gains in the proportion of students who reached the proficient and advanced categories in language at the grade level. These percentages were highly substantial, indicating great performance of the multiple regression models in accounting for the variance in gains in the proportion of students who reached the proficient and advanced categories in both mathematics and ELA at the grade level.

DISCUSSION

Summary of Principal Findings

We set out to develop an instrument that researchers and practitioners can use to measure, evaluate, and understand school renewal efforts.

This task was guided by a theoretical underpinning that distinguishes between school reform and school renewal. We asked the question whether it is possible to develop an instrument that can uniquely capture school renewal efforts. We also specifically emphasized the critical importance of school teachers to any school renewal efforts. As a result, our goal was to develop a concise instrument that researchers and practitioners can practically apply to address various aspects of school renewal efforts from the perspective of school teachers. We performed multiple comparisons of CFAs to confirm the structural validity of our original specification of twenty-one activities (i.e., items) representing seven aspects of school renewal efforts. After confirming the factorial validity, we continued to examine the internal consistencies of the instrument and its seven factors or dimensions and found a high level of reliability. We found that the instrument has sound factorial validity and reliability.

We continued to test the ability of our instrument to predict school academic performance and meanwhile investigated the relationship between school academic performance and school renewal efforts. We examined separately how the seven dimensions and the whole measure of school renewal efforts were associated with school academic performance, controlling for school contextual characteristics. We found that school renewal efforts (dimensions and the whole measure) were able to predict school academic performance in M-STEP (both mathematics and ELA). To a somewhat lesser degree, we found that school renewal efforts (dimensions and the whole measure) could also predict gains in school academic performance in M-STEP (both mathematics and ELA) (from the previous year to the current year). Our multiple regression models that produced these results indicated rather acceptable performance.

In terms of the relationship between school academic performance in M-STEP and school renewal efforts, we identified D1 (Focus on students and their achievement), D7 (Internal responsibility), and D2 (Continuous school improvement) in this order as the leading dimensions of school renewal efforts that were most strongly related to school academic performance in mathematics and D7 (Internal responsibility) as the leading dimension of school renewal efforts that was most strongly related to school academic performance in ELA.

Meanwhile, we identified D1 (Focus on students and their achievement), D3 (Balance between the internal and external influences), and D2 (Continuous school improvement) in this order as the leading dimensions of school renewal efforts that were most strongly related to gains in school academic performance in mathematics and D7 (Internal responsibility and professionalism) as the leading dimension of school renewal efforts that was most strongly related to gains in school academic performance in ELA.

A Reliable and Valid Instrument to Measure School Renewal

The research reported in this chapter has the purpose to develop and validate an instrument measuring school leadership. The psychometric testing indicates that the seven-factor structure is a valid and reliable way to measure the efforts of school renewal. Given the sound validation results, it is appropriate to emphasize two advantages of our instrument. First, the instrument is concise. With only twenty-one items on the instrument, it is easy and convenient to apply, increasing the chance of a high return (rate) given the length of the instrument. Second, the instrument is comprehensive. With seven factors or dimensions, the instrument covers major aspects of school renewal efforts. The instrument can be used as an aggregated whole measure of school renewal efforts, or specific dimensions of school renewal efforts can be selected for focused research and evaluation. In general, researchers and practitioners can easily use the instrument to collect valid and reliable data to measure, evaluate, and understand school renewal efforts.

Prediction of School Performance

Our instrument was developed to measure, evaluate, and understand school renewal efforts from the perspective of school teachers. Such a perspective emphasizes the critical importance of school teachers in any effort of school renewal. In an instrument validation study, we were able to show good reliability and validity of the instrument. From the psychometric perspective, the present study attempted to examine the ability of the instrument to predict, perhaps, the most important outcome of school renewal efforts, school academic performance. We observed interesting properties of the instrument in making predictions of school academic performance. We found that the instrument is sensitive to M-STEP measures. M-STEP measures included static measures on the proportion of students who reached the proficient and advanced categories in mathematics and language at the grade level (i.e., the within grade proportion) and gain measures on the increase in the proportion of students who reached the proficient and advanced categories in mathematics and language at the grade level (from the previous year to the current year). M-STEP is a state assessment program with examination questions closely matching curriculum standards. In other words, M-STEP is a content- or curriculum-based assessment. Our finding in the present study therefore indicates that the instrument is sensitive to the content- or curriculum-based performance.

Priority of School Renewal

From a practical perspective, we applied our instrument to investigate the relationship between school academic performance and school renewal efforts. The following discussion focuses on M-STEP because a significant relationship emerged between M-STEP-related school academic performance and school renewal efforts. Although all dimensions of school renewal efforts were important to school academic performance, we found that some dimensions were more strongly related to school academic performance than others. The priority of school renewal efforts to school academic performance can be appreciated from two perspectives.

First, there are more dimensions of school renewal efforts that stand out as the leading predictors of school academic performance in mathematics than in language (three versus one in both static measures and gain measures). Also, it is evident in Tables 5.4 and 5.5 that dimensions and the whole measure of school renewal efforts tend to relate more strongly to school academic performance in mathematics than in ELA. In some psychometric language, our instrument tends to be more sensitive to school academic performance in mathematics than in ELA.

Second, there are consistent dimensions of school renewal efforts that claim "leadership" across school academic performance (static and gain) measures. In terms of mathematics, they are D1 (Focus on students and their achievement) and D2 (Continuous school improvement). In terms of ELA, it is D7 (Internal responsibility and professionalism). Across mathematics and ELA, it is D7 (Internal responsibility and professionalism). Therefore, we have identified at least three dimensions of school renewal efforts that are worthy of attention. This finding is consistent with a growing body of evidence on the relationship between school leadership activities and student performance: Focus on students and their achievement has been found to be a key difference between high achieving schools and low performing schools (Bamburg & Andrews, 1991; R. D. Goddard et al., 2000), and positively related to better student performance (Nunnery et al., 2011; Osborne-Lampkin et al., 2015). Continuous school improvement has positive influence on student achievement growth (Campbell & Levin, 2009; Gallimore et al., 2009; Heck & Hallinger, 2009) and long-term academic performance (Stringfield et al., 2008). The internal responsibility is related to both student math and reading achievement (Sweetland & Hoy, 2000) and a key to the Finland success in Programme for International Student Assessment (Sahlberg, 2011). These three dimensions together portray the efforts of school teachers who take responsibility in and hold themselves accountable for continuous school improvement aimed at students and their academic performance. Such coordinated efforts tend to relate strongly with school academic performance in ELA and particularly in mathematics. Therefore, we recommend that policymakers, school administrators, and school teachers pay close attention to these leading dimensions of school renewal efforts (without ignoring the other dimensions because they too contribute to school academic performance). These school renewal efforts tend to penetrate effectively from the school level to the student level in strong association with academic performance of students as a whole.

Implications for Researchers, Policymakers, and Practitioners

The present study has implications for educational researchers, Policymakers and practitioners. For researchers, our study offers a new framework for school improvement. We provide new evidence on factorial validity, reliability and predictive power of the school renewal instrument. For policymakers, our study, among many other things, has again proved the effectiveness of the key elements of renewal model. Therefore, the renewal model should be encouraged in policy and practice. For practitioners, since the dimensions of *Orientation to School Renewal* come from the literature and several years of discussion with principals and teachers in the field as they were engaged in school renewal activities (see Shen & Burt, 2015; Shen & Cooley, 2013), it is a practitioner-friendly, and ready-to-use tool for schools to monitor quality of school improvement efforts.

Guidance for Improvement from the "Process" Perspective

The framework of seven dimensions of school renewal provides some guidance for the "process" perspective. There are two related aspects to the school improvement process – the "content" and "process" of the improvement. If the learning-centered leadership in the previous chapter offers some advice from the "content" perspective, the seven-dimension school renewal framework offers some guidance from the "process" perspective. School professionals could engage in these process-oriented activities to initiate and sustain school renewal. Focusing on both the "content" and "process" of school improvement is a key element for the school renewal model.

APPENDIX 5.1: ORIENTATION TO SCHOOL RENEWAL: AN INSTRUMENT

Dimension 1. Focus on students and their achievement

01   Our school improvement process is guided strongly by the goal of improving student achievement.

02   Our school truly has high expectations for all students.

03   All teachers have a clear, shared vision about expectations for all students.

(*cont.*)

Dimension 2. Continuous school improvement

04 Our school has a continuous focus on teaching and learning.

05 All our teachers continuously seek ways to enhance the teaching and learning processes.

06 Our school consistently uses a continuous improvement process/strategy, rather than starting from scratch for each initiative.

Dimension 3. Balance between the internal and external influences

07 We openly welcome ideas and input on school improvement from all stakeholders.

08 We successfully balance external pressure and internal initiative for school improvement.

09 We successfully prioritize our school improvement efforts despite competing priorities.

Dimension 4. The dialogue, decision, action and evaluation (DDAE) model

10 We consistently dialogue in our school about our school improvement priorities.

11 Our school improvement strategies are well coordinated within the school.

12 Our school successfully monitors the progress of our school improvement initiatives with data.

Dimension 5. Implementation integrity

13 We consistently monitor our data and develop school improvement initiatives accordingly.

14 We have a clear process in place to continuously generate new ideas for school improvement.

15 We consistently re-prioritize school improvement efforts based on continuous data updates.

Dimension 6. Implementers as active developers

16 Our school really decides our school improvement priorities.

17 We usually develop our own programs for school improvement (rather than buying from an external vendor).

18 We consistently adapt and adjust existing programs based on our outcome data.

Dimension 7. Internal responsibility and professionalism

19 We all hold ourselves and each other accountable.

20 We all hold our students accountable for their own achievement.

21 Continuous reflection on school improvement is part of our professional culture.

APPENDIX 5.2: THREE MEASUREMENT MODELS FOR THE CONSTRUCT OF "SCHOOL RENEWAL"

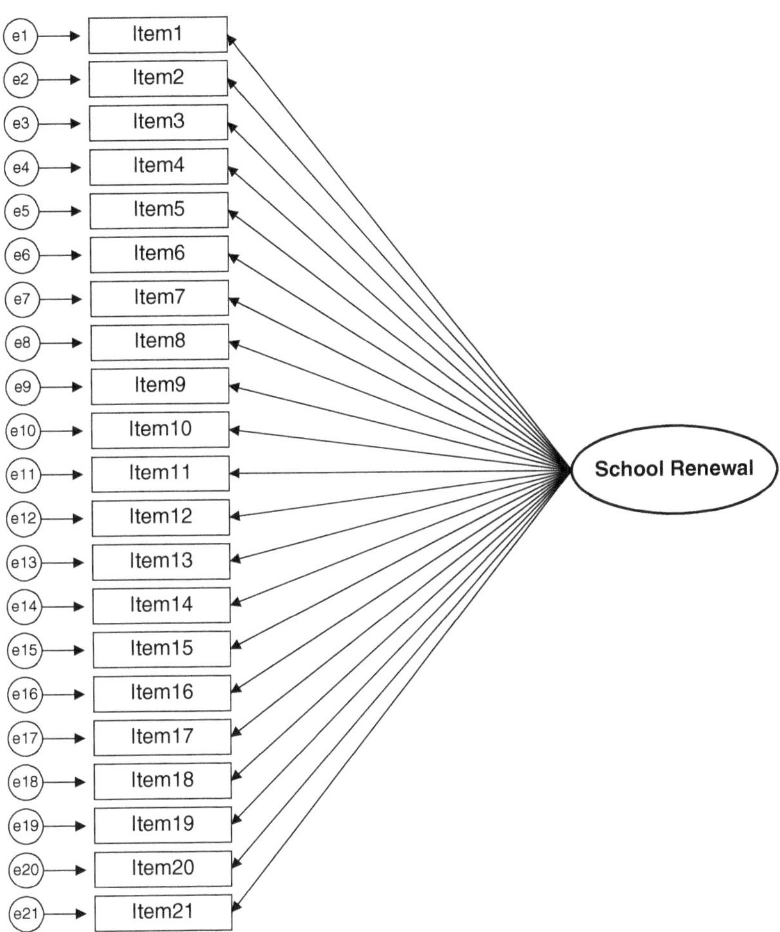

A.5.2.1 The one-factor model

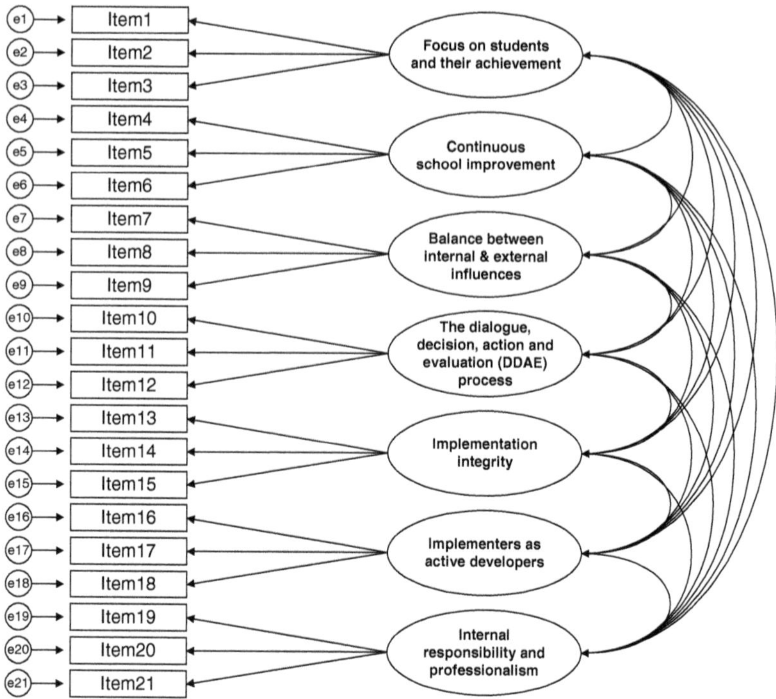

A.5.2.2 The seven-factor model

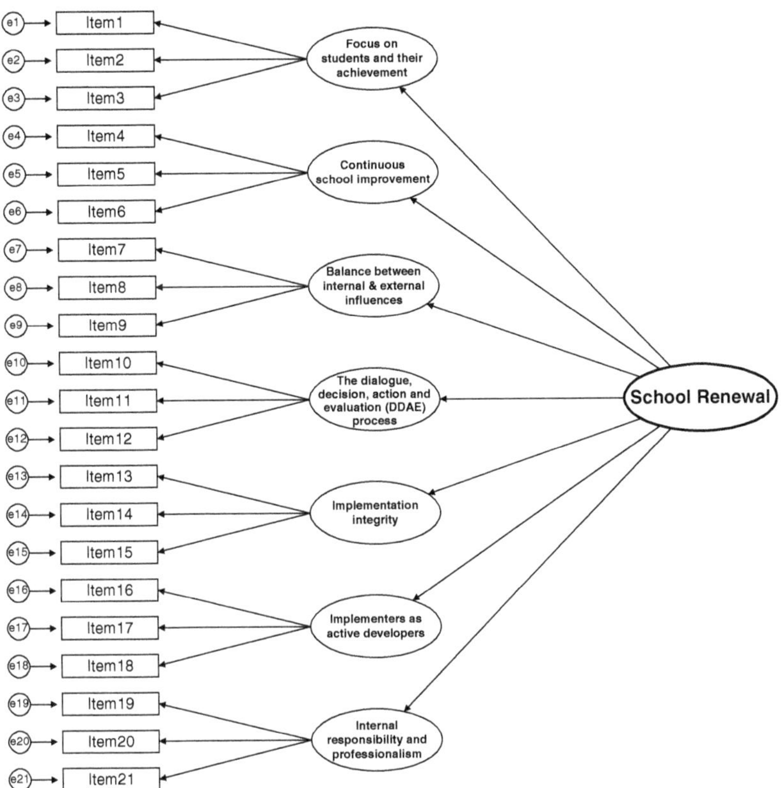

A.5.2.3 The model of seven factors with one higher-order factor

CHAPTER 6

Toward the School Renewal Model

THE SCHOOL RENEWAL MODEL: A BRIEF SUMMARY

The school renewal model was built on two key basic empirical findings – one on the structural nature of the educational system and the other on the relationship between principal and teacher leadership. First, the educational system in the US is found to be bifurcated with a fault line between the state-district-school tectonic plate and the classroom tectonic plate, rather than loosely coupled throughout the system. This finding on the structural nature of the educational system points to the importance of prioritizing bridging the fault line between the two tectonic plates in school improvement efforts. Second, the relationship between principal and teacher leadership is predominantly a win-win situation rather than a zero-sum game. In other words, leadership in schools is expandable, rather than a pie with a fixed size. This finding points to the importance of utilizing, enhancing, and integrating principal leadership and teacher leadership to bridge the fault line.

Since the fault line is within the school – an organic whole as an organization, the school becomes a critical unit in school renewal. Educational changes range from the macro-level (such as federal or state policies) to the micro-level (such as coaching a teacher for teaching literacy using a new method). School as a critical unit for change, at the meso-level, (a) incorporates the pressure and demand from the macro level, (b) bridges the fault line between the state-district-school tectonic plate and the classroom tectonic plate, and (c) creates conducive conditions for micro-level changes. School renewal is a model that considers and capitalizes on the two significant findings on the bifurcated nature of the educational system and the win-win relationship between principal and teacher leadership, and advocates for a way of school improvement focusing on the integrated school leadership, a model that differs from the traditional reform model.

How could the principal and teachers in a school work together to overcome the fault line and improve the school outcomes by engaging in the school renewal model? This book offers one way to operationalize the school renewal model. The operationalization focuses on both the "content" and "process" of school renewal. As far as the content is concerned, Chapter 4 offers a validated framework of integrated, learning-centered school leadership. The integrated learning-centered school leadership is an instrument that has sound psychometric properties. The seven dimensions could be mutually distinguished from each other. The tool has sound internal consistency as indicated by Cronbach's alpha, a reliability measure. The ratings on the integrated learning-centered school leadership are associated with school-level student achievement. Therefore, the integrated, learning-centered school leadership framework provides the contents for school renewal, that is, seven content dimensions that the principal and teachers could engage in together, as a way to bridge the fault line.

As to the "process" of school renewal, Chapter 5 offers a validated framework of Orientation to School Renewal, including seven "process" dimensions in which the principal and teachers could engage jointly. The framework of "Orientation to School Renewal" also has sound psychometric properties as an instrument. The seven dimensions could be mutually distinguished from each other. The tool has sound internal consistency as indicated by Cronbach's alpha, a reliability measure. The ratings on the Orientation to School Renewal are associated with not only the school-level student achievement for the current year but also the gain in school-level student achievement from the prior year to the current year. Therefore, the Orientation to School Renewal framework provides a process for school renewal, that is, seven process dimensions that the principal and teachers could engage in together, as a way to overcome the bifurcation in the educational system.

Many of the reform agendas either focus on the "content" (such as a particular reading program) or the "process" (such as a step-by-step guide for school improvement). Under the renewal model, it is important to emphasize both the content areas in which the principal and teachers could work together and the process through which the principal and teachers could engage jointly. Bridging the fault line from both the "content" and "process" perspectives offers more ways for the principal and teachers to integrate their leadership to bridge the fault line. It is important to point out that the integrated, learning-centered school leadership framework as the content, and the orientation to the school renewal framework as the process, as illustrated in Chapters 4 and 5, are one way to operationalize the school renewal. Other frames and practices could be developed under the school renewal model.

LEADERSHIP DENSITY AND SCHOOL RENEWAL

At the heart of the school renewal model is enhancing the leadership density in our schools. Traditionally, school leadership equals principal leadership. In the context of school renewal, emphasizing principal leadership is necessary but not sufficient. Based on the current research, the framework of leadership density in schools has at least the following four inter-related components: (a) principal leadership, (b) teacher leadership, (c) the relationship between the principal and teacher leadership, and (d) the relationship among teachers. The idea of four-component leadership density in schools could be expanded and strengthened as more practice and research contribute to a more encompassing vision of school leadership.

Principal Leadership

There is a mature body of research that investigates the effects of principal leadership on school outcomes, including student achievement, and the pathways along which the effects take place. For example, as early as 1987, Andrews and Soder (1987) analyzed the relationship between principal leadership and student achievement based on two years of data from a school district and concluded that principal leadership was crucial for ensuring student achievement, particularly for vulnerable children. Later on, Marzano et al. (2005) conducted meta-analyses and distilled twenty-one principal leadership responsibilities associated with student achievement, answering the questions *what* principals should do. Other scholars studied *how* principals could make an impact. For example, Hallinger and Heck (1996) identified that principal leadership could have direct effects, indirect effects, moderated effects, mediated effects, reciprocal effects, etc., on school outcomes. Leithwood et al. (2010, 2020) proposed the four-path model, that is, principals' influence on student learning via the emotional, rational, organizational, and familial paths.

There have been efforts in recent years to quantify the effect size of principals' influence on student achievement and other school outcomes (e.g., Grissom, 2021; Hitt & Tucker, 2016; Liebowitz & Porter, 2019; Wu & Shen, 2022; Shen & Wu, 2024). Wu and Shen (2022) conducted a meta-meta-analysis and found that principal leadership has a statistically significant positive relationship with student achievement, with an effect size Cohen's d of 0.34. More recently, Shen and Wu (2024) conducted a multivariate meta-analysis of forty-two studies published between 2000 and 2020 in the US, and found that principal leadership had a positive and significant effect on student achievement when the effects were conceptualized as direct effects without controls (0.25 SD) or as indirect effects (0.22 SD). The research evidence suggests that both what principals do and how they do it are associated with school outcomes. Principal leadership is an important part of the framework of leadership density in schools for the renewal model.

Teacher Leadership

There has been a burgeoning literature base that demonstrates the effectiveness of teacher leadership. One group of the literature on teacher leadership focuses on the dimensions of teacher leadership that are associated with better school outcomes, including student achievement. For example, the meta-analysis by Shen et al. (2020) found that teacher leadership as an overall practice has a small positive relationship with student achievement ($r = .19$); they also estimated the effect sizes for the following seven dimensions of teacher leadership: (a) promoting shared vision, mission and goals of student learning ($r = .18$), (b) coordinating and managing beyond the classroom ($r = .18$), (c) facilitating improvement in curriculum, instruction and assessment ($r = .21$), (d) promoting teachers' professional development ($r = .19$), (e) engaging in policy and decision-making ($r = .18$), (f) improving outreach and collaboration with families and communities ($r = .15$), and (g) fostering a collaborative culture in school ($r = .17$).

There are various definitions of teacher leadership and different ways to structure teacher leadership (Nguyen et al., 2020; York-Barr & Duke, 2004). How teacher leadership is structured is related to its effectiveness. For example, Sands (2024) studied the effects of the New York City Department of Education's Teacher Career Pathways program (a teacher leadership program) on student achievement in grades three to eight. She used a method called difference-in-difference, an analysis technique that could infer causality. She found that in schools where teacher leaders were staffed into "formal roles with defined responsibilities, positional authority, and commensurate salary increases," there was an improvement in academic achievement in both English language arts and mathematics. She also found that the improvement accelerated over time. Schools where teacher leadership was structured more formally in terms of roles, authority, and compensation had increasing gains over the years. Schools that did not staff teacher leaders from the program did not have similar results. It appears that both what teacher leaders do and the structure in which they exercise teacher leadership are related to school outcomes. Therefore, teacher leadership provides another avenue to increase leadership density for school renewal.

The Win-Win Relationship between Principal Leadership and Teacher Leadership

The win-win relationship between principal and teacher leadership has been discussed in Chapter 3. Empirical findings based on national data indicate that the leadership relationship between the principal and teachers is primarily characterized by the win-win situation, rather than the zero-sum game (Shen & Xia, 2012; Xia & Shen, 2020), an insight that points to the third avenue – beyond principal leadership and teacher leadership – to increase the density of leadership in schools. Principal leadership and teacher leadership could leverage and enhance each other not only to increase the leadership density in schools but also to bridge the fault line in the bifurcated educational system.

The Relationship among Teachers

The fourth avenue for increasing the leadership density in schools is to improve the relationship among teachers, which is an extension of teacher leadership. Lortie's (1975) classic study underscores the complexities of teacher interactions, revealing that while only a small proportion of educators (25 percent) frequently engage with colleagues, a majority (54 percent) perceive knowledge-sharing as a key aspect of collegiality. Despite this recognition, the ways in which teachers collaborate remain varied and are often conflated in academic discourse. Three primary teacher-to-teacher relationship frameworks – professional learning communities (PLCs), teacher collaboration, and teacher networks – have been identified in the literature (de Lima, 2001; Hargreaves, 2001; Little, 1990; Lomos et al., 2011). However, scholars often use these terms interchangeably due to the lack of clear distinctions among them (Adams, 2000; Schuster et al., 2021; Swindler, 2009). While some researchers, such as Muijs et al. (2011), explore aspects of these frameworks, there is limited discussion on their intersections and differences. Each framework offers a distinct perspective: PLCs emphasize shared norms and collective professional growth, teacher collaboration focuses on joint work toward common goals, and teacher networks examine the depth and breadth of professional connections among educators.

Zheng et al.'s (2024) meta-analysis revealed the effects of the three types of teacher-to-teacher relationships on student achievement. The impact of these teacher relationships on student achievement varies across levels of interaction. Individual teacher relationships were not directly linked to student outcomes, whereas connections within schools or grade-level teams showed significant positive correlations with student performance in mathematics and reading. At the broader organizational level, all three frameworks demonstrated small, but positive associations with math achievement, with teacher collaboration ($r = .191$), teacher network ($r = .202$), and PLC ($r = .189$) yielding similar results. However, their effects on reading achievement differed, with teacher networks having the strongest correlation ($r = .290$), followed by teacher collaboration ($r = .163$) and PLCs ($r = .078$). These findings suggest that overall the types of teacher-to-teacher relationships at an organizational level, rather than at the individual level, are associated with student achievement.

The meta-analysis findings indicate that the relationship among teachers at the organizational level is another avenue to increase the leadership density in schools to facilitate school renewal.

In summary, to support school renewal, enhancing leadership density requires moving beyond the traditional focus on principal leadership to a broader, multi-faceted framework. This framework includes four inter-related components: (a) **principal leadership**, which remains foundational and is shown to have direct, indirect, and other effects on school outcomes; (b) **teacher leadership**, which contributes to school improvement through specific practices and is most effective when structured formally with clear roles and authority; (c) the **relationship between principal leadership and teacher leadership**, which operates as a win-win dynamic where both roles reinforce each other, rather than compete; and (d) the **relationship among teachers**, which encompasses collaboration, networks, and PLCs – all of which, particularly at the organizational level, are positively linked to student achievement. Together, these four avenues offer an encompassing and impactful vision of leadership density, essential for advancing school renewal efforts.

OTHER STAKEHOLDERS' ROLES IN FACILITATING SCHOOL RENEWAL

Policymakers' Role

Policymakers at the federal, state, and local levels could also play a role in facilitating school renewal. First, policymakers should design policies that support integrated leadership at the school level. Policymakers should craft policies that explicitly encourage collaboration between the principal and teachers, recognizing the expandable nature of school leadership. Rather than simply mandating top-down reforms, policies should incentivize shared decision-making at the school level. For example, policies could be created to reward schools that demonstrate effective principal-teacher collaboration aligned with student learning goals. Research by Honig and Rainey (2023) emphasizes that successful school improvement often depends on district leaders enabling the principal and teachers to take shared leadership roles within their schools. This approach aligns with Darling-Hammond et al. (2017), who argue that instructional leadership is most impactful when distributed and embedded in collaborative school cultures.

Second, policymakers should create flexible, context-sensitive implementation guidelines. Federal and state education policies often fail because they are rigid and detached from local contexts. To support the school renewal model, policymakers should move away from one-size-fits-all mandates and instead provide adaptable frameworks that allow school communities to customize implementation strategies. These guidelines should be rooted in local data and include room for innovation, reflection, and adjustment. For example, Darling-Hammond (2010) calls for adaptive policies that trust educators' professional judgment in implementing reforms suited to their contexts.

Third, policymakers should rebalance accountability measures to encourage internal responsibility. Current policies often emphasize external accountability through high-stakes testing and performance audits. While accountability is important, an overemphasis on compliance can suppress innovation and demotivate educators. Policymakers should rebalance accountability frameworks to also recognize internal responsibility and professionalism. Darling-Hammond and Snyder (2015) argue that professional accountability – built on professional capacity and other factors – produces more sustainable improvement than punitive external systems. Reframing accountability to include evidence of collaborative leadership practices and data-informed improvement processes aligns with the school renewal model's emphasis on internal responsiveness.

Finally, policymakers, particularly the policymakers at the school district level, should support capacity building at the school level through sustained and coordinated professional development. Effective implementation of the school renewal model requires informed, capable educators. The district should ensure that professional development programs are designed to build teacher and principal capacity simultaneously, fostering a common language and shared goals. Darling-Hammond et al. (2017) emphasize that high-quality professional learning is essential for change efforts that lead to real improvements in teaching and learning. Spillane and Coldren (2015) stress that capacity building in schools must be grounded in the distributed nature of leadership, where leadership functions are not solely confined to the principal but are spread across multiple actors within the school system, including teachers and others. Under the school renewal model, professional development is not just about individual skill acquisition, but also about building organizational capacity for collaborative decision-making and instructional improvement.

Researchers' Role

Researchers could play a role in facilitating school renewal as well. First, as Goodlad (1975) pointed out, researchers must move away from the paradigm of "research, development, dissemination, and evaluation (RDDE)" as characterized in the school reform model. The RDDE paradigm is flawed because it does not consider many factors in educational change, particularly the fault line in the bifurcated educational system. It is a fallacy to assume that educational change is all about simply "disseminating" research-based programs or practices, because whether the research-based program or practice is appropriate for the unique situation of the school and classroom needs to be decided first. Furthermore, the cultural, political, organizational, and other implementation-related factors could also complicate the presumably linear "dissemination" process. As argued previously in the book for the school renewal model, beginning with implementation integrity – let the principal and teachers decide what is the most impactful to pursue given the current unique conditions in the school – is a more motivating approach to school improvement.

Second, following the discussion in the previous section on "leadership density in schools," it is important for researchers to investigate ways to increase the leadership density in schools for school renewal. What are the areas in which the principal and teachers could work together to improve school outcomes? What are the efficient and effective strategies to integrate principal leadership and teacher leadership? In addition to the four avenues to increasing leadership density in schools, are there any other avenues based on the voice from the field and related research? The research and knowledge on increasing leadership density in schools would facilitate the school renewal model tremendously.

Third, the school renewal model, supported by the bifurcation theory and the win-win theory, also points to other areas for research to generate knowledge for the practice of school renewal. For example, the notion of mentoring or coaching would be different under the renewal model and under the reform model because under the renewal model mentoring and coaching have to be more contextualized, facilitate the balance between the external pressure and internal response, and motivate school personnel to engage in continuous improvement by being active developers rather than passive recipients. The notion of school-university partnership would also take on a new meaning and warrants additional research so that university personnel will not just produce "package programs" and leave at the school door. Effective ways for university personnel to facilitate school renewal are among the important areas to study.

CODA: TWO VIEWS ON MOVING TOWARD THE SCHOOL RENEWAL MODEL

Based on the experience with principals and teachers on funded projects, there appear to be two views and practices regarding moving toward the school renewal model. The first view holds that, due to the governance structure of the US educational system, schools will continue to face externally driven mandates. As a result, the school reform model will remain in place. For those who take this view, they tend to believe that the school reform and school renewal models will coexist in practice, and the important thing is that the percentage of the practices characterized by the school renewal model increases. The first view essentially treats the school reform and renewal models as two parallel models. The second view is to treat the school renewal model as an overarching model that not only has merits in its own right but also is a way to assimilate the reform model. Since the school renewal model emphasizes "balancing the external pressure and internal responsiveness," engages in the "dialogue, decision, action, evaluation" process, treats "implementers as developers," and does these as part of the "internal responsibility and professionalism," all externally driven reform agendas will be internalized and implemented via the school renewal model. Therefore, the second view treats the school renewal model as an overarching model that could internalize the externally driven reform agenda and generate renewal initiatives based on the internal responsiveness.

When recruiting schools for the three funded projects for school renewal – Learning-Centered Leadership Development Program, Achievement-Centered Leadership Development Program, and Developing a Leadership Pipeline and Turning Around Schools Simultaneously, our project team explained to potential participating schools that the school renewal model does not add more work to their already crowded plate; rather, the school renewal model would facilitate an overall approach to school improvement efforts. Among others, we encouraged the principal and teachers of the participating schools to use a tool called "school renewal matrix" to develop renewal initiatives that take into account both externally driven agendas and internal responsiveness (Shen & Burt, 2015). There has been positive feedback from the personnel in the participating schools of the three projects on using the school renewal model as an overarching approach to school improvement. In moving toward the school renewal model, we hope to see a transition from viewing school reform and school renewal as two parallel models to viewing the school renewal model as an overarching approach to school improvement that could internalize and incorporate the reform agenda. The education profession writ large – including policymakers, practitioners, researchers, and others – still has much to learn in order to renew our schools.

References

Adams, J. (2000). *Taking charge of curriculum: Teacher networks and curriculum implementation.* Teachers College Press.

Aguayo, R. (1990). *Dr. Deming: The American who taught the Japanese about quality.* New Fireside.

Allen, N., Grigsby, B., & Peters, M. L. (2015). Does leadership matter? Examining the relationship among transformational leadership, school climate, and student achievement. *NCPEA International Journal of Educational Leadership Preparation, 10*(2), 1–22.

Anderson, S., Leithwood, K., & Strauss, T. (2010). Leading data use in schools: Organizational conditions and practices at the school and district levels. *Leadership and Policy in Schools, 9*(3), 292–327.

Andrews, R. L., & Soder, R. (1987). Principal leadership and student achievement. *Educational Leadership, 44*(6), 9–11.

Angelle, P. S., & Schmid, J. B. (2007). School structure and the identity of teacher leaders: Perspectives of principals and teachers. *Journal of School Leadership, 17*(6), 771–799.

Bamburg, J. D., & Andrews, R. L. (1991). School goals, principals, and achievement. *School Effectiveness and School Improvement, 2*(3), 175–191.

Barab, S. A., & Luehmann, A. L. (2003). Building sustainable science curriculum: Acknowledging and accommodating local adaptation. *Science Education, 87,* 454–467.

Barr, J. (2016). *Developing a positive classroom climate.* IDEA Paper #61, IDEA Center, Inc.

Barth, R. S. (1990). *Improving schools from within: Teachers, parents, and principals can make the difference.* Jossey-Bass.

Bejar, I. (2008). Standard setting: What is it? Why is it important? *ETS R&D Connections, 7,* 1–6.

Bentler, P. M. (1990). Comparative fit indexes in structural models. *Psychological Bulletin, 107,* 238–246.

Bentler, P. M., & Bonett, D. G. (1980). Significance tests and goodness-of-fit in the analysis of covariance structures. *Psychological Bulletin, 88,* 588–606.

Berkovich, I. (2016). School leaders and transformational leadership theory: Time to part ways? *Journal of Educational Administration, 54*(5), 609–622. https://doi.org/10.1108/JEA-11-2015-0100

Berman, P., & McLaughlin, M. W. (1976). Implementation of educational innovation. *The Education Forum, 40,* 345–370.

Bernhardt, V. (2004). *Data analysis for continuous school improvement.* Eye on Education.

Bernhardt, V. (2009). *Data, data everywhere: Bringing all the data together for continuous school improvement.* Eye on Education.

Bitter, C., O'Day, J. O., Gubbins, P., & Socias, M. (2009). What works to improve student literacy achievement? An examination of instructional practices in a balanced literacy approach. *Journal of Education for Students Placed at Risk (JESPAR), 14*(1), 17–44. https://doi.org/10.1080/10824660802715403

Black, P., & Wiliam, D. (1998). Assessment and classroom learning. *Assessment in Education, 5,* 7–74.

Blase, J., & Blase, J. (1999). Principals' instructional leadership and teacher development: Teachers' perspectives. *Educational Administration Quarterly, 35*(3), 349–378.

Blase, J., & Blase, J. (2000). Effective instructional leadership: Teachers' perspectives on how principals promote teaching and learning in schools. *Journal of Educational Administration, 38*(2), 130–141.

Blasé, J., & Blasé, J. (2001). *Empowering teachers: What successful principals do?* (2nd ed.). Corwin Press, Inc.

Blasé, J., & Kirby, P. (Eds.). (2008). *Bringing out the best in teachers: What effective principals do?* (3rd ed.). Corwin Press.

Boberg, J. E., & Bourgeois, S. J. (2016). The effects of integrated transformational leadership on achievement. *Journal of Educational Administration, 54*(3), 357–374.

Boles, K., & Troen, V. (1994). Teacher leadership in a professional development school. Paper presented at the Annual Meeting of the American Educational Research Association, New Orleans, LA, April 4–8. Retrieved from www.eric.ed.gov/

Bond, G., Evans, R., Salyers, L., Williams, M., & Kim, P. (2000). Measurement of fidelity in psychiatric rehabilitation. *Mental Health Services Research, 2*(2), 75–87.

Bowers, A. J. (2020). *Examining a congruency-typology model of leadership for learning using two-level latent class analysis with TALIS 2018.* Organisation for Economic Co-operation and Development, Paris, France. https://doi.org/10.1787/c963073b-en

Boykin, A. W., & Cunningham, R. T. (2001). The effects of movement expressiveness in story content and learning context on the analogical reasoning performance of African American children. *Journal of Negro Education, 70*(1–2), 72–83.

Brewer, D. J. (1993). Principals and student outcomes: Evidence from US high schools. *Economics of Education Review, 12*(4), 281–292.

Bryk, A. S. (2016, March 17). Fidelity of implementation: Is it the right concept? Carnegie Foundation for the Advancement of Teaching. Retrieved from www.carnegiefoundation.org/blog/fidelity-of-implementation-is-it-the-right-concept/

Bryk, A. S., Gomez, L. M., & Grunow, A. (2010). *Getting ideas into action: Building networked improvement communities in education.* Carnegie Foundation for the Advancement of Teaching. Retrieved from www.carnegiefoundation.org/spotlight/webinar-bryk-gomez-building-networked-improvement-communities-in-education

Bryk, A. S., Sebring, P. B., Allensworth, E., Luppescu, S., & Easton, J. (2009). *Organizing schools for improvement: Lessons from Chicago.* University of Chicago Press.

Campbell, C., & Levin, B. (2009). Using data to support educational improvement. *Educational Assessment. Evaluation and Accountability, 21*(1), 47–65. https://doi.org/10.1007/s11092-008-9063-x

Campbell, C., Lieberman, A., Yashkina, A., Alexander, S., & Rodway, J. (2018). *Teacher learning and leadership program: Research report 2017–18.* Ontario Teachers' Federation.

Carbaugh, B. G., Marzano, R. J., & Toth, M. D. (2015). *Leadership for results: Shifting the focus of leader evaluation.* West Palm Beach, FL: Learning Sciences International.

Carlson, D., Borman, G. D., & Robinson, M. (2011). A multistate district-level cluster randomized trial of the impact of data-driven reform on reading and mathematics achievement. *Educational Evaluation and Policy Analysis, 33*(3), 378–389. https://doi.org/10.3102/0162373711412765

Carroll, C., Patterson, M., Wood, S., Booth, A., Rick, J., & Balain, S. (2007). A conceptual framework for implementation fidelity. *Implementation Science, 2*(1), 40.

Celio, M. B., & Harvey, J. (2005). *Buried treasure: Developing a management guide from mountains of school data.* Center on Reinventing Public Education.

Century, J., & Cassata, A. (2016). Implementation research: Finding common ground on what, how, why, where, and who. *Review of Research in Education, 40,* 169–215.

Cerych, L. (1997). Educational reforms in Central and Eastern Europe: Processes and Outcomes. *European Journal of Education, 32*(1), 75–96.

Chang, I.-H. (2011). A study of the relationships between distributed leadership, teacher academic optimism, and student achievement in Taiwanese elementary schools. *School Leadership & Management, 31*(5), 491–515.

Chapman, C. (2008). Towards a framework for school-to-school networking in challenging circumstances. *Educational Research, 50*(4), 403–420.

Chapman, C., & Muijs, D. (2014). Does school-to-school collaboration promote school improvement? A study of the impact of school federations on student outcomes. *School Effectiveness and School Improvement, 25*(3), 351–393.

Clark, L. A., & Watson, D. (1995). Constructing validity: Basic issue in objective scale development. *Psychological Assessment, 7*, 309–319.

Clune, W. H. (1993). The best path to systemic educational policy: Standard/centralized or differentiated/decentralized. *Educational Evaluation and Policy Analysis, 15*, 233–254.

Coburn, C. E., & Turner, E. O. (2012). The practice of data use: An introduction. *American Journal of Education, 118*(2), 99–111.

Cohen, D. K. (1990). A revolution in one classroom: The case of Mrs. Oublier. *Educational Evaluation and Policy Analysis, 12*(3), 311–329.

Cohen, D. K. (1995). What is the system in systemic reform? *Educational Researcher, 24*(9), 11–17.

Cohen, D. K. (2011, August 31). Predicaments of reform [Online post]. Retrieved from www.shankerinstitute.org/blog/predicaments-reform

Cotton, K. (2003). *Principals and student achievement: What the research says.* ASCD.

Covey, S. R. (1989). *The seven habits of highly effective people: Restoring the character ethic.* Simon & Schuster.

Crowther, F., Kaagen, S. S., Ferguson, M., & Hann, L. (2002). *Developing teacher leaders: How teacher leadership enhances school success.* Corwin Press.

Crum, K. S., & Sherman, W. H. (2008). Facilitating high achievement: High school principals' reflections on their successful leadership practices. *Journal of Educational Administration, 46*(5), 562–580.

Cuban, L. (1990). Reforming again, again, and again. *Educational Researcher, 19*(1), 3–13.

Dane, A. V., & Schneider, B. H. (1998). Program integrity in primary and early secondary prevention: Are implementation effects out of control? *Clinical Psychology Review, 18*(1), 23–45.

Daniëls, E., Hondeghem, A., & Dochy, F. (2019). A review on leadership and leadership development in educational settings. *Educational Research Review, 27*(2019), 110–125.

Darling-Hammond, L. (2010). *The flat world and education: How America's commitment to equity will determine our future.* Teachers College Press.

Darling-Hammond, L., & Snyder, J. (2015). Meaningful learning in a new paradigm for educational accountability: An introduction. *Education Policy Analysis Archives, 23*, 1–4.

Darling-Hammond, L., Ancess, J., & Ort, S. W. (2002). Reinventing high school: Outcomes of the coalition campus school project. *American Educational Research Journal, 39*(3), 639–673.

Darling-Hammond, L., Bullmaster, M. L., & Cobb, V. L. (1995). Rethinking teacher leadership through professional development schools. *The Elementary School Journal, 96*(1), 87–106.

Darling-Hammond, L., Hyler, M. E., & Gardner, M. (2017). *Effective teacher professional development.* Learning Policy Institute. www.learningpolicyinstitute .org/sites/default/files/product-files/Effective_Teacher_Professional_ Development_REPORT.pdf

Datnow, A., & Hubbard, L. (2015). Teacher capacity for and beliefs about data-driven decision making: A literature review of international research. *Journal of Educational Change, 17*(1), 7–28. https://doi.org/10.1007/s10833-015-9264-2

Datnow, A., & Park, V. (2018). *Professional collaboration with purpose: Teacher learning towards equitable and excellent schools.* Routledge.

Day, C., Gu, Q., & Sammons, P. (2016). The impact of leadership on student outcomes: How successful school leaders use transformational and instructional strategies to make a difference. *Educational Administration Quarterly, 52*(2), 221–258.

de Lima, D. C. (2001). English-as-a-foreign-language teacher-training programs: An overview. *Revista Linguagem & Ensino, 4*(2), 143–153.

Deal, T. E., & Celotti, L. D. (1980). How much influence do (and can) educational administrators have on classrooms? *The Phi Delta Kappan, 61*(7), 471–473.

Deming, W. E. (1986). *Out of the crisis.* Cambridge, MA: MIT Center for Advanced Engineering Study.

Diamond, J. B., & Cooper, K. (2007). The uses of testing data in urban elementary schools: Some lessons from Chicago. *Teachers College Record, 109*(13), 241–263.

Dill, E. M., & Boykin, A. W. (2000). The comparative influence of individual, peer tutoring, and communal learning contexts on the text recall of African American children. *Journal of Black Psychology, 26*(1), 65–78.

DuFour, R. (2004). What is a "professional learning community"? *Educational Leadership, 61*(8), 6–11.

Dutta, V., & Sahney, S. (2016). School leadership and its impact on student achievement. *International Journal of Educational Management, 30*(6), 941–958.

Eberts, R. W., & Stone, J. A. (1988). Student achievement in public schools: Do principals make a difference? *Economics of Education Review, 7*(3), 291–299.

Egan, D., & Marshall, S. (2007). Educational leadership and school renewal in Wales. *Australian Journal of Education, 51*(3), 286–298.

Elmore, R. F. (2000). *Building a new structure for school leadership.* Albert Shanker Institute.

Firestone, W. (2009). Accountability nudges districts into changes in culture. *Phi Delta Kappan, 90,* 670–676.

Firestone, W. A., & Wilson, B. L. (1985). Using bureaucratic and cultural linkages to improve instruction: The principal's contribution. *Educational Administration Quarterly, 21*(2), 7–30.

Fixsen, D. L., Blasé, K. A., Duda, M., Naoom, S. F., & Van Dyke, M. (2010). Sustainability of evidence-based programs in education. *Journal of Evidence-Based Practices for Schools, 11*(1), 30–46.

Fixsen, D. L., Naoom, S. F., Blase, K. A., Friedman, R. M., & Wallace, F. (2005). *Implementation research: A synthesis of the literature.* University of South Florida, Louis de la Parte Florida Mental Health Research Institute, The National Implementation Research Network.

Fogleman, J., McNeill, K. L., & Krajcik, J. (2011). Examining the effect of teachers' adaptations of a middle school science inquiry-oriented curriculum unit on student learning. *Journal of Research in Science Teaching, 48*(2), 149–169.

Forbes, C. T., & Davis, E. A. (2010). Curriculum design for inquiry: Preservice elementary teachers' mobilization and adaptation of science curriculum materials. *Journal of Research in Science Teaching, 47,* 820–839.

Fowler, F. C. (2009). *Policy studies for educational leaders: An introduction* (3rd ed.). Boston: Pearson.

Friedkin, N. E., & Slater, M. R. (1994). School leadership and performance: A social network approach. *Sociology of Education, 67*(2), 139–157.

Fuhrman, S. H. (1993a) (Ed.). *Designing coherent education policy: Improving the system.* San Jossey-Bass.

Fuhrman, S. H. (1993b). The politics of coherence. In S. H. Fuhrman (Ed.), *Designing coherent policy: Improving the system* (pp. 1–34). Jossey-Bass.

Fullan, M. (2007). Educational reform as continuous improvement. In W. Hawley (Ed.), *The keys to effective schools: Educational reform as continuous improvement* (pp. 1–12). Corwin, CA: Thousand Oaks.

Fullan, M. G. (1994). Teacher leadership: A failure to conceptualize. In *Archives of Phi Delta Kappa International, Readings on leadership in education* (pp. 109–124). Phi Delta Kappa Educational Foundation.

Fusarelli, L. D. (2002). Tightly coupled policy in loosely coupled systems: Institutional capacity and organizational change. *Journal of Educational Administration, 40*(6), 561–575.

Fusarelli, L. D. (2005). Gubernatorial reactions to No Child Left Behind: Politics, pressure, and education reform. *Peabody Journal of Education, 80*(2), 120–136.

Gallimore, R., Ermeling, B. A., Saunders, W. M., & Goldenberg, C. (2009). Moving the learning of teaching closer to practice: Teacher education implications of school-based inquiry teams. *Elementary School Journal, 109*(5), 537–553.

Garet, M. S., Wayne, A. J., Stancavage, F., Taylor, J., Walters, K., Song, M., Brown, S., Hurlburt, S., Zhu, P., Sepanik, S., & Doolittle, F. (2010). *Middle school mathematics professional development impact study: Findings after the first year of implementation (NCEE 2010-4009).* National Center for Education Evaluation and Regional Assistance, Institute of Education Sciences, U.S. Department of Education.

REFERENCES

Garvin, D. A. (1993). Building a learning organization. *Harvard Business Review, 71*, 78–91.

Garvin, D. A., Edmondson, A. C., & Gino, F. (2008, March). Is yours a learning organization? *Harvard Business Review, 86*(3), 109–116.

George, D., & Mallery, M. (2010). *SPSS for Windows step by step: A simple guide and reference* (10th ed.). Pearson.

Glass, G. V., & Hopkins, K. D. (1996). *Statistical methods in psychology and education* (3rd ed.). Allyn & Bacon.

Goddard, R. D. (2001). Collective efficacy: A neglected construct in the study of schools and student achievement. *Journal of Educational Psychology, 93*, 467–476.

Goddard, R. D., Goddard, Y., Kim, E. S., & Miller, R. (2015). A theoretical and empirical analysis of the roles of instructional leadership, teacher collaboration, and collective efficacy beliefs in support of student learning. *American Journal of Education, 121*(4), 501–530.

Goddard, R. D., Hoy, W. K., & Hoy, A. W. (2004). Collective efficacy beliefs: Theoretical developments, empirical evidence, and future directions. *Educational Researcher, 33*(3), 1–13.

Goddard, R. D., Sweetland, S. R., & Hoy, W. K. (2000). Academic emphasis of urban elementary schools and student achievement in reading and mathematics: A multilevel analysis. *Educational Administration Quarterly, 36*(5), 683–702. https://doi.org/10.1177/00131610021969164

Goddard, Y. L., Goddard, R. D., Bailes, L. P., & Nichols, R. (2019). From school leadership to differentiated instruction a pathway to student learning in schools. *Elementary School Journal, 120*(2), 198–219.

Goddard, Y. L., Goddard, R. D., & Tschannen-Moran, M. (2007). A theoretical and empirical investigation of teacher collaboration for school improvement and student achievement in public elementary schools. *Teachers College Record, 109*(4), 877–896.

Goldspink, C. (2007). Rethinking educational reform: A loosely coupled and complex systems perspective. *Educational Management Administration & Leadership, 35*(1), 27–50.

Goodlad, J., Klein, M. F., & Associates. (1975). *Looking behind the classroom door.* Charles A. Jones Publishing Company.

Goodlad, J. I. (1975a). Schools can make a difference. *Educational Leadership, 33*, 108–117.

Goodlad, J. I. (1975b). *The uses of alternative views of educational change (The Phi Delta Kappa Meritorious Award Monograph).* Phi Delta Kappa.

Goodlad, J. I. (1999). Flow, eros, and ethos in educational renewal. *Phi Delta Kappan, 80*(8), 571–578.

Goodlad, J. I., & Klein, M. F. (1970). *Behind the classroom door.* Charles. A. Jones Pub. Co.

Gordon, S. P., Smyth, J., & Diehl, J. (2008). The Iraq War, "sound science," and "evidence-based" educational reform: How the Bush administration uses deception, manipulation, and subterfuge to advance its chosen ideology. *Journal for Critical Education Policy Studies, 6*(2), 173–204.

Grissom, J., Egalite, A. J., & Lindsay, C. A. (2021). *How principals affect students and schools: A systematic synthesis of two decades of research.* The Wallace Foundation. Retrieved from www.wallacefoundation.org/principalsynthesis

Grossman, P. L., & Stodolsky, S. S. (1995). Content as context: The role of school subjects in secondary school teaching. *Educational Researcher, 24*(8), 5–11.

Gunal, Y., & Demirtasli, R. (2016). A pathway to educational accountability: The relationship between effective school characteristics and student achievement. *Universal Journal of Educational Research, 4*(9), 2049–2054.

Gunter, H. M., & Fitzgerald, T. (2013). New public management and the modernization of education systems. *Journal of Educational Administration and History, 45*(3), 213–219. https://doi.org/10.1080/00220620.2013.796914

Hallinger, P. (2003). Leading educational change: Reflections on the practice of instructional and transformational leadership. *Cambridge Journal of Education, 33*(3), 329–351.

Hallinger, P., & Heck, R. H. (1996a). The principal's role in school effectiveness: An assessment of methodological progress, 1980–1995. In K. Leithwood & P. Hallinger (Eds.), *International handbook of educational leadership and administration* (pp. 723–783). Kluwer Academic Publishers.

Hallinger, P., & Heck, R. H. (1996b). Reassessing the principal's role in school effectiveness: A review of empirical research, 1980–1995. *Educational Administration Quarterly, 32*(1), 5–44. https://doi.org/10.1177/0013161X96032001002

Hallinger, P., & Heck, R. H. (1998). Exploring the principal's contribution to school effectiveness: 1980–1995. *School Effectiveness and School Improvement, 9*(2), 157–191.

Hallinger, P., & Heck, R. H. (2010a). Collaborative leadership and school improvement: Understanding the impact on school capacity and student learning. *School Leadership & Management, 30*(2), 95–110. https://doi.org/10.1080/13632431003663214

Hallinger, P., & Heck, R. H. (2010b). Leadership for learning: Does collaborative leadership make a difference in school improvement? *Educational Management Administration & Leadership, 38*(6), 654–678.

Hallinger, P., & Heck, R. H. (2011a). Conceptual and methodological issues in studying school leadership effects as a reciprocal process. *School Effectiveness and School Improvement, 22*(2), 149–173.

Hallinger, P., & Heck, R. H. (2011b). Exploring the journey of school improvement: Classifying and analyzing patterns of change in school improvement processes and learning outcomes. *School Effectiveness and School Improvement, 22*(1), 1–27.

Halverson, R., Grigg, J., Prichett, R., & Thomas, C. (2007). The new instructional leadership: Creating data-driven instructional systems in school. *Journal of School Leadership, 17*(2), 159–194.

Handler, B. (2010). Teacher as curriculum leader: A consideration of the appropriateness of that role assignment to classroom-based practitioners. *International Journal of Teacher Leadership, 3*(3), 32–42.

Hanuscin, D. L., Cheng, Y. W., Rebello, C., Sinha, S., & Muslu, N. (2014). The affordances of blogging as a practice to support ninth-grade science teachers' identity development as leaders. *Journal of Teacher Education, 65*(3), 207–222.

Hanushek, E. A., & Raymond, M. E. (2005). Does school accountability lead to improved student performance? *Journal of Policy Analysis and Management, 24*(2), 297–327.

Hargreaves, A. (2001). The emotional geographies of teachers' relations with colleagues. *International Journal of Educational Research, 35*(5), 503–527. https://doi.org/10.1016/S0883-0355(02)00006-X

Harris, A. (2005). Teacher leadership: More than just a feel-good factor? *Leadership and Policy in Schools, 4*(3), 201–219.

Harris, A., & Hopkins, D. (1999). Teaching and learning and the challenge of educational reform. *School Effectiveness and School Improvement, 10*(2), 257–267.

Harris, A., & Hopkins, D. (2000). Introduction to special feature: Alternative perspectives on school improvement. *School Leadership & Management, 20*(1), 9–14.

Harris, A., & Jones, M. (2010). Professional learning communities and system improvement. *Improving Schools, 13*(2), 172–181.

Harris, A., & Muijs, D. (2003). *Teacher leadership: A review of the research.* National College for School Leadership.

Harris, A., & Young, J. (2000). Comparing school improvement programs in England and Canada. *School Leadership & Management, 20*(1), 31–42. https://doi.org/10.1080/13632430068860

Harris, A., Jones, M., & Huffman, J. (2017). *Teachers leading educational reform: The power of professional learning communities.* Routledge.

Hautala, T., Helander, J., & Korhonen, V. (2018). Loose and tight coupling in educational organizations – An integrative literature review. *Journal of Educational Administration, 56*(2), 236–258.

Heck, R. H. (1992). Principals' instructional leadership and school performance: Implications for policy development. *Educational Evaluation and Policy Analysis, 14*(1), 21–34.

Heck, R. H., & Hallinger, P. (2009). Assessing the contribution of distributed leadership to school improvement and growth in math achievement. *American Educational Research Journal, 46*(3), 659–689. https://doi.org/10.3102/0002831209340042

Heck, R. H., & Hallinger, P. (2010). Collaborative leadership effects on school improvement: Integrating unidirectional- and reciprocal-effects models. *Elementary School Journal, 111*(2), 226–252.

Heck, R. H., & Hallinger, P. (2014). Modeling the longitudinal effects of school leadership on teaching and learning. *Journal of Educational Administration, 52*(5), 653–681.

Heck, R. H., & Marcoulides, G. A. (1993). Principal leadership behaviors and school achievement. *NASSP Bulletin, 77*(553), 20–28.

Hess, F. M., & Fullerton, J. (2009). The numbers we need: Bringing balanced scorecards to education data. *Phi Delta Kappan, 90*(9), 665–669.

Hitt, W. D. (1995). The learning organization: Some reflections on organizational renewal. *Leadership & Organization Development Journal, 16*(8), 17–25. https://doi.org/10.1108/01437739510097996

Hitt, D. H., & Tucker, P. D. (2016). Systematic review of key leader practices found to influence student achievement: A unified framework. *Review of Educational Research, 86*(2), 531–569. https://doi.org/10.3102/0034654315614911

Honig, M. I., & Coburn, C. (2008). Evidence-based decision making in school district central offices: Toward a policy and research agenda. *Educational Policy, 22*(4), 578–608.

Honig, M. I., & Hatch, T. C. (2004). Crafting coherence: How schools strategically manage multiple, external demands. *Educational Researcher, 33*(8), 16–30.

Honig, M. I., & Rainey, L. R. (2023). *From tinkering to transformation.* Harvard Education Press.

Hopinks, D. (2013). Exploding the myths of school reform. *School Leadership & Management, 33*(4), 304–321.

Hopkins, D., Harris, A., & Jackson, D. (1997). Understanding the school's capacity for development: Growth states and strategies. *School Leadership & Management, 17*(3), 401–411.

Hox, J. J., & Maas, C. J. (2001). The accuracy of multilevel structural equation modeling with pseudobalanced groups and small samples. *Structural Equation Modeling, 8*(2), 157–174.

Hsieh, C., & Shen, J. (1998). Teachers', principals', and superintendents' perceptions of leadership. *School Leadership and Management, 18*(1), 107–121.

Hu, L., & Bentler, P. M. (1999). Cutoff criteria for fit indexes in covariance structure analysis: Conventional criteria versus new alternatives. *Structural Equation Modeling, 6,* 1–55.

Hulleman, C. S., & Cordray, D. S. (2009). Moving from the lab to the field: The role of fidelity and achieved relative intervention strength. *Journal of Research on Educational Effectiveness, 2,* 88–110. https://doi.org/10.1080/19345740802539325

Ingersoll, R. M. (1993). Loosely coupled organizations revisited. *Research in the Sociology of Organizations, 11*, 81–112.

Ingersoll, R. M. (1994). Organizational control in secondary schools. *Harvard Educational Review, 64*(2), 150–172.

Ingersoll, R. M. (1996). Teachers' decision-making power and school conflict. *Sociology of Education, 69*(2), 159–176.

Ingersoll, R. M. (2003). *Who controls teachers' work?* Harvard University Press.

Ingram, D., Louis, K. S., & Schroeder, R. G. (2004). Accountability policies and teacher decision making: Barriers to the use of data to improve practice. *Teachers College Record, 106*(6), 1258–1287.

Jackson, C. K., Wigger, C., & Xiong, H. (2021). Do school spending cuts matter? Evidence from the Great Recession. *American Economic Journal: Economic Policy, 13*(2), 304–335.

Jacob, R., Goddard, R., Kim, M., Miller, R., & Goddard, Y. (2015). Exploring the causal impact of the McREL Balanced Leadership Program on leadership, principal efficacy, instructional climate, educator turnover, and student achievement. *Educational Evaluation and Policy Analysis, 37*(3), 314–332. https://doi.org/10.3102/0162373714549620

Jacques, C., & Potemski, A. (2014). *21st century educators: Developing and supporting great career and technical education teachers.* American Institute for Research, Center on Great Teachers and Leaders.

Jimerson, J. B., & McGhee, M. W. (2013). Leading inquiry in schools: Examining mental models of data-informed practice. *Current Issues in Education, 16*(1), 1–22.

Johnson, P. A. (2013). Effective board leadership: Factors associated with student achievement. *Journal of School Leadership, 23*(3), 456–489.

Johnson, P. E., & Short, P. M. (1998). Principal's leader power, teacher empowerment, teacher compliance and conflict. *Educational Management & Administration, 26*(2), 147–159.

Joyce, B., & Calhoun, E. (1995). School renewal: An inquiry, not a formula. *Educational Leadership, 52*(7), 51–55.

Joyce, B., Wolf, J., & Calhoun, E. (1993). *The self-renewing school,* Alexandria, VA: ASCD.

Kanter, R. M. (1994). Power failure in management circuits. In L. Mainiero & C. Tromley (Eds.), *Developing managerial skills in organizational behavior: Exercises, cases, and reading* (pp. 322–329). Prentice Hall.

Katzenmeyer, M., & Moller, G. (2009). *Awakening the sleeping giant: Helping teachers develop as leaders* (3rd ed.). Corwin Press.

Kauermann, G., & Carroll, R. J. (2001). A note on the efficiency of sandwich covariance matrix estimation. *Journal of the American Statistical Association, 96*(456), 1387–1396.

Keiser, N. M., & Shen, J. (2000). Principals' and teachers' perceptions of teacher empowerment. *Journal of Leadership Studies, 7*(3), 115–121.

Kline, P., & Saunders, B. (1998). *Ten steps to a learning organization* (2nd ed.). Arlington, VA: Great Ocean Publishers.

Kouzes, J. M., & Posner, B. Z. (1987). *The leadership challenge: How to get extraordinary things done in organizations.* Jossey-Bass.

Ladson-Billings, G. (1994). *The dreamkeepers: Successful teachers of African American children.* Jossey-Bass.

Ladson-Billings, G. (1995a). Toward a theory of culturally relevant pedagogy. *American Educational Research Journal, 32*(3), 465–491.

Ladson-Billings, G. (1995b). But that's just good teaching? The case for culturally relevant pedagogy. *Theory into Practice, 34*(3), 159–165.

Ladson-Billings, G. (1998). Teaching in dangerous times: Culturally relevant approaches to teacher assessment. *The Journal of Negro Education, 67*(3), 255–267.

Lai, M. K., & McNaughton, S. (2016). The impact of data use professional development on student achievement. *Teaching and Teacher Education, 60,* 434–443.

Lee, J., & Wong, K. K. (2004). The impact of accountability on racial and socioeconomic equity: Considering both school resources and achievement outcomes. *American Educational Research Journal, 41,* 797–832.

Lee, V., & Smith, J. B. (1996). Collective responsibility for learning and its effects on gains in achievement and engagement for early secondary school students. *American Journal of Education, 104*(2), 103–147.

Leithwood, K., & Jantzi, D. (1999). The relative effects of principal and teacher sources of leadership on student engagement with school. *Educational Administration Quarterly, 35*(5), 679–706.

Leithwood, K., & Jantzi, D. (2000). Principal and teacher leadership effects: A replication. *School Leadership and Management, 20*(4), 415–434.

Leithwood, K., & Jantzi, D. (2005). A review of transformational leadership research, 1996–2005. *Leadership and Policy in Schools, 4*(3), 177–200.

Leithwood, K., & Jantzi, D. (2006). Transformational school leadership for large scale reform: Effects on students, teachers and their classroom practices. *School Effectiveness and School Improvement, 17*(2), 201–228.

Leithwood, K., & Jantzi, D. (2008). Linking leadership to student learning: The contributions of leader efficacy. *Educational Administration Quarterly, 44*(4), 496–528.

Leithwood, K., & Louis, K. S. (2011). *Linking leadership to student learning* (1st ed.). Jossey-Bass.

Leithwood, K., & Sun, J. (2012). The nature and effects of transformational school leadership: A meta-analytic review of unpublished research. *Educational Administration Quarterly, 48*(3), 387–423.

Leithwood, K., Louis, K. S., Anderson, S., & Wahlstrom, K. (2004). *Review of research: How leadership influences student learning.* The Wallace Foundation.

REFERENCES

Leithwood, K., Patten, S., & Jantzi, D. (2010). Testing a conception of how school leadership influences student learning. *Educational Administration Quarterly, 46*(5), 671–706. https://doi.org/10.1177/0013161X10377347

Leithwood, K., Sun, J., & Schumacker, R. (2020). How school leadership influences student learning: A test of "The Four Paths Model." *Educational Administration Quarterly, 56*(4), 570–599. https://doi.org/10.1177/0013161X19878772

LeMahieu, P. (2011, October 11). What we need in education is more integrity (and less fidelity) of implementation. Carnegie Foundation for the Advancement of Teaching. Retrieved from www.carnegiefoundation.org/blog/what-we-need-in-education-is-more-integrity-and-less-fidelity-of-implementation/

Lewis, A. C. (2002). A horse called NCLB. *Phi Delta Kappan, 84*(3), 179–180.

Lezotte, L. W. (1991). *Correlates of effective schools: The first and second generations.* Okemos, MI: Effective Schools Products, Ltd.

Liebowitz, D. D., & Porter, L. (2019). The effect of principal behaviors on student, teacher, and school outcomes: A systematic review and meta-analysis of the empirical literature. *Review of Educational Research, 89*(5), 785–827. https://doi.org/10.3102/0034654319866133

Little, J. (1990). The persistence of privacy: Autonomy and initiative in teachers. *Teachers College Record, 91*(4), 509–536. https://doi.org/10.1177/016146819009100403

Little, J. W. (1985). Teachers as teacher advisors: The delicacy of collegial leadership. *Educational Leadership, 43*(3), 34–36.

Little, J. W. (2012). Understanding data use practice among teachers: The contribution of micro-process studies. *American Journal of Education, 118*(2), 143–166.

Lomos, C., Hofman, R. H., & Bosker, R. J. (2011). Professional communities and student achievement – A meta-analysis. *School Effectiveness and School Improvement, 22*(2), 121–148. https://doi.org/10.1080/09243453.2010.550467

Lortie, D. C. (1975). *Schoolteacher: A sociological study.* University of Chicago Press.

Louis, K. S. (2006). Changing the culture of schools: Professional community, organizational learning, and trust. *Journal of School Leadership, 16,* 477–489.

Louis, K. S., Leithwood, K., Wahlstrom, K. L., & Anderson, S. E. (2010). *Investigating the links to improved student learning: Final report of research findings.* University of Minnesota. Retrieved from www.cehd.umn.edu/carei/Leadership/Learning-from-Leadership_Final-Research-Report_July-2010.pdf

Louis, K. S., & Marks, H. M. (1998). Does professional community affect the classroom? Teachers' work and student experiences in restructuring schools. *American Journal of Education, 106*(4), 532–575.

Louis, K. S., Marks, H. M., & Kruse, S. D. (1996). Teachers' professional community in restructuring schools. *American Journal of Education, 33*(4), 757–798.

Lundahl, L., Arreman, I. E., Lundström, U., & Rönnberg, L. (2010). Setting things right? Swedish upper secondary school reform in a 40-year perspective. *European Journal of Education, 45*(1), 46–59.

Lutz, F. W. (1982). Tightening up loose coupling in organizations of higher education. *Administrative Science Quarterly, 27*(4), 653–669.

MacCallum, R. C., Widaman, K. F., Zhang, S., & Hong, S. (1999). Sample size in factor analysis. *Psychological Methods, 4*(1), 84–99.

Malen, B., & Cochran, M. V. (2008). Beyond pluralistic patterns of power: Research on the micropolitics of schools. In B. S. Cooper, J. G. Cibulka, & L. D. Fusarelli (Eds.), *Handbook of education politics and policy* (pp. 148–178). Routledge.

Mandinach, E. B., Honey, M., & Light, D. (2006, April). A theoretical framework for data-driven decision making. In *The annual meeting of the American Educational Research Association, San Francisco, CA* (pp. 39–52).

Mangin, M. M. (2005). Distributed leadership and the culture of schools: Teacher leaders' strategies for gaining access to classrooms. *Journal of School Leadership, 15*(4), 456–484.

Manthey, G. (2006). Collective efficacy: Explaining school achievement. *Leadership, 35*(3), 23, 36.

Marks, H. M., & Louis, K. S. (1997). Does teacher empowerment affect the classroom? The implications of teacher empowerment for instructional practice and student academic performance. *Educational Evaluation and Policy Analysis, 19*(3), 245–275.

Marks, H. M., Louis, K. S., & Printy, S. (2000). The capacity for organizational learning: Implications for pedagogy and student achievement. In K. Leithwood (Ed.), *Organizational learning and school improvement* (pp. 239–266). JAI.

Marks, H. M., & Printy, S. M. (2003). Principal leadership and school performance: An integration of transformational and instructional leadership. *Educational Administration Quarterly, 39*(3), 370–397.

Marsh, J. A., Bertrand, M., & Huguet, A. (2015). Using data to alter instructional practice: The mediating role of coaches and professional learning communities. *Teachers College Record, 117*, 1–40.

Marzano, R. J., Waters, T., & McNulty, B. A. (2005). *School leadership that works.* Association for Supervision and Curriculum Development.

Mason, S. A. (2001). Turning data into knowledge: Lessons from six Milwaukee public schools. Using data for educational decision making. *Newsletter of the Comprehensive Center-Region VI, 6*, 3–6.

Mason, S. A. (2003). Learning from data: The role of professional learning communities. Paper presented at the *2003 annual meeting of the American Educational Research Association*, Chicago, IL.

McCoach, D. B. (2010). Hierarchical linear modeling. In G. R. Hancock, R. O. Mueller, & L. M. Stapleton (Eds.), *The reviewer's guide to quantitative methods in the social sciences* (pp. 123–140). Routledge.

McDermott, K. A., & Jensen, L. S. (2005). Dubious sovereignty: Federal conditions of aid and the No Child Left Behind Act. *Peabody Journal of Education, 80*(2), 39–56.

McGuinn, P. (2005). The national schoolmarm: No Child Left Behind and the new educational federalism. *Publius, 35*(1), 41–68.

McPartland, J. M. (2011). Organizing Schools for Improvement: Lessons from Chicago. *Contemporary Sociology, 40*(1), 16.

Meyer, J. W., & Rowan, B. (1978). The structure of educational organizations. In J. W. Meyer (Ed.), *Environments and organizations* (pp. 78–109). Jossey-Bass.

Meyer, J. W., & Rowan, B. (1992). The structure of educational organization. In J. W. Meyer & W. R. Scott (Eds.), *Organizational environment: Ritual and rationality* (pp. 71–97). Sage.

Michelli, N. M. (2016). The National Network for Educational Renewal and the legacy of John Goodlad. *Kappa Delta Pi Record, 52*(4), 148–149.

Michigan Council for Educator Effectiveness. (2013). Building an improvement-focused system of educator evaluation in Michigan. Retrieved from www.static1.squarespace.com/static/577fc4e2440243084a67dc49/t/578cf74fe6f2e1c03c0d8207/1468856149186/MCEE_final+recommendations_full+report.pdf

Mitchell, C., & Sackney, L. (2011). *Profound improvement: Building learning-community capacity on living-system principles.* Routledge.

Moolenaar, N. M., Sleegers, P. J. C., & Daley, A. J. (2012). Teaming up: Linking collaboration networks, collective efficacy, and student achievement. *Teaching and Teacher Education, 28*(2), 251–262.

Morley, L., & Rassool, N. (2000). School effectiveness: New managerialism, quality and the Japanization of education. *Journal of Education Policy, 15*(2), 169–183.

Muijs, D., & Harris, A. (2003). Teacher leadership-improvement through empowerment? An overview of the literature. *Educational Management & Administration, 31*(4), 437–448.

Muijs, D., & Harris, A. (2006). Teacher led school improvement: Teacher leadership in the UK. *Teaching and Teacher Education, 22*(8), 961–972.

Muijs, D., Ainscow, M., Chapman, C., & West, M. (2011). *Collaboration and networking in education.* Springer Science & Business Media.

Murphy, J. (2005). *Connecting teacher leadership and school improvement.* Corwin Press.

National Policy Board for Educational Administration. (2015). *Professional standards for educational leaders 2015.* Author.

Neufeldt, V. (Ed.). (1991). *Webster's new world dictionary of American English* (3rd college ed.). Simon & Schuster.

REFERENCES

Newmann, F. E., Smith, B., Allensworth, E., & Bryk, A. S. (2001). Instructional program coherence: What it is and why it should guide school improvement policy. *Educational Evaluation and Policy Analysis, 23,* 297–321.

Nguyen, D., Harris, A., & Ng, D. (2020). A review of the empirical research on teacher leadership (2003–2017): Evidence, patterns and implications. *Journal of Educational Administration, 58*(1), 60–80.

Nolan, B., & Palazzolo, L. (2012). New teacher perceptions of the "teacher leader" movement. *NASSP Bulletin, 95*(4), 302–318.

Nunnally, J. C., & Bernstein, I. H. (1994). *Psychometric theory* (3rd ed.). McGraw-Hill.

Nunnery, J. A., Ross, S. M., Chappell, S., Pribesh, S., & Hoag-Carhart, E. (2011). *The impact of the NISL Executive Development Program on school performance in Massachusetts: Cohort 2 results.* Center for Educational Partnerships, Darden College of Education, Old Dominion University.

O'Day, J. A. (2002). Complexity, accountability, and school improvement. *Harvard Educational Review, 72*(3), 293–329.

O'Day, J. A., & Smith, M. S. (1993). Systemic change and educational opportunity. In S. H. Fuhrman (Ed.), *Designing coherent policy: Improving the system* (pp. 250–312). Jossey-Bass.

Orton, J. D., & Weick, K. E. (1990). Loosely coupled systems: A reconceptualization. *Academy of Management Review, 15*(2), 203–223.

O'Donnell, R. J., & White, G. P. (2005). Within the accountability era: Principal instructional leadership behaviors and student achievement. *NASSP Bulletin, 89*(645), 56–72.

Osborne-Lampkin, L., Folsom, J. S., & Herrington, C. D. (2015). *A systematic review of the relationships between principal characteristics and student achievement* (REL 2016-091). Washington, DC: U.S. Department of Education, Institute of Education Sciences, National Center for Education Evaluation and Regional Assistance, Regional Educational Laboratory Southeast.

Owens, R. G., & Valesky, T. C. (2007). *Organizational behavior in education: Adaptive leadership and school reform.* Allyn and Bacon.

Pajak, E., & Green, A. (2003). Loosely coupled organizations, misrecognition, and social reproduction. *International Journal of Leadership in Education, 6*(4), 393–413.

Parsons, T. (1963). On the concept of political power. *Proceedings of the American Philosophical Society, 107*(3), 232–262.

Phillips, J. (2003). Powerful learning: Creating learning communities in urban school reform. *Journal of Curriculum and Supervision, 18*(3), 240–258.

Pont, B., Nusche, D., & Moorman, H. (2008). *Improving school leadership, Volume 1: Policy and practice.* Paris: OECD.

Poppink, S. (2015). Lessons from eight schools: Leadership teams and direction from a school renewal activities matrix. In J. Shen & W. Burt (Eds.), *Learning-centered school leadership: School renewal in action* (pp. 189–207). Peter Lang.

Porter, A. C., Polikoff, M. S., Goldring, E., Murphy, J., Elliott, S. N., & May, H. (2010). Developing a psychometrically sound assessment of school leadership: The VAL-ED as a case study. *Educational Administration Quarterly, 46*(2), 135–173.

Portin, B. (2004). The roles that principals play. *Educational Leadership, 61*(7), 14–18.

Portin, B., & Shen, J. (2005). The changing principalship. In J. Shen (Ed.), *School principals.* Peter Lang.

Pounder, D. G. (1995). Leadership as an organization-wide phenomenon: Its impact on school performance. *Educational Administration Quarterly, 31*(4), 564–588.

Rafferty, A. E., & Griffin, M. A. (2004). Dimensions of transformational leadership: Conceptual and empirical extensions. *The Leadership Quarterly, 15*(3), 329–354.

Raudenbush, S. W., & Bryk, A. S. (2001). *Hierarchical linear models: Applications and data analysis methods* (2nd ed.). Newbury Park, CA: Sage.

Reeves, D. B. (2008). *Reframing teacher leadership to improve your school.* Association for Supervision and Curriculum Development.

Reeves, P., Palmer, L. B., McCrumb, D., & Shen, J. (2014). Sustaining a renewal model for school improvement. In K. L. Sanzo (Ed.), *From policy to practice: Sustainable innovations in school leadership preparation and development* (pp. 267–292). Charlotte, NC: Information Age Publication.

Rhodes, J. E., Camic, P. M., Milburn, M., & Lowe, S. R. (2009). Improving middle school climate through teacher-centered change. *Journal of Community Psychology, 37*(6), 711–724.

Roberts-Gray, C., Gingiss, P. M., & Boerm, M. (2007). Evaluating school capacity to implement new programs. *Evaluation and Program Planning, 30*(3), 247–257. https://doi.org/10.1016/j.evalprogplan.2007.04.002

Robinson, V. M., Lloyd, C. A., & Rowe, K. J. (2008). The impact of leadership on student outcomes: An analysis of the differential effects of leadership types. *Educational Administration Quarterly, 44*(5), 635–674.

Rodriguez-Campos, L., Rincones-Gomez, R., & Shen, J. (2008). Do teachers, principals, and superintendents perceive leadership the same way: A structural equation modeling test of a multi-dimensional construct across groups. *Frontiers of Education in China, 3*(3), 360–385.

Rosenthal, R., & Rosnow, R. L. (2008). *Essentials of behavioral research: Methods and data analysis.* McGraw-Hill.

Rowan, B. (2002). Rationality and reality in organizational management: Using the coupling metaphor to understand educational (and other) organizations – A concluding comment. *Journal of Educational Administration, 40*(6), 604–611.

Rudner, L. M., & Boston, C. (2003). Data warehousing: Beyond disaggregation. *Educational Leadership, 60*(5), 62–65.

Rux, P. P. (1998). Decisions, decisions, decisions! *Book Report, 17*(1), 31.

Sahlberg, P. (2011). *Finnish lessons: What can the world learn from educational change in Finland?* Teachers College Press.

Sands, S. R. (2024). *Democratic policymaking in schools: The influence of teacher empowerment on student achievement.* EdWorkingPaper No. 24-989. Brown University.

Sarason, S. (1982). *The culture of the school and the problem of change* (2nd ed.). Allyn & Bacon.

Sarason, S. (1990). *The predictable failure of educational reform: Can we change course before it's too late?* Jossey-Bass.

Scheerens, J. (2012). Summary and conclusion: Instructional leadership in schools as loosely coupled organizations. In J. Scheerens (Ed.), *School leadership effects revisited: Review and meta-analysis of empirical studies* (pp. 131–152). Springer.

Schildkamp, K., & Poortman, C. L. (2015). Factors influencing the functioning of data teams. *Teachers College Record, 117*, 1–42.

Schrum, L., & Levin, B. B. (2013). Leadership for Twenty-First-Century schools and student achievement: Lessons learned from three exemplary cases. *International Journal of Leadership in Education, 16*(4), 379–398.

Schuster, J., Hartmann, U., & Kolleck, N. (2021). Teacher collaboration networks as a function of type of collaboration and schools' structural environment. *Teaching and Teacher Education, 103.* https://doi.org/10.1016/j.tate.2020.103372

Sebastian, J., Allensworth, E., & Huang, H. (2016). The Role of Teacher Leadership in How Principals Influence Classroom Instruction and Student Learning. *American Journal of Education, 123*(1), 69–108.

Sebastian, J., Huang, H., & Allensworth, E. (2017). Examining integrated leadership systems in high schools: Connecting principal and teacher leadership to organizational processes and student outcomes. *School Effectiveness and School Improvement, 28*(3), 463–488.

Sebring, P. B., & Bryk, A. S. (2000). School leadership and the bottom line in Chicago. *Phi Delta Kappan, 81*(6), 440–443.

Senge, P. M. (1990). *The fifth discipline: The art and practice of the learning organization.* New York: Bantam Doubleday Dell.

Senge, P. M., Cambron-McCabe, N., Lucas, T., Smith, B., Dutton, J., & Kleiner, A. (2012). *Schools that learn: A fifth discipline fieldbook for educators, parents, and everyone who cares about education* (Rev. ed.). New York, NY: Crown Business.

Senge, P. M., Lichtenstein, B. B., Kaeufer, K., Bradbury, H., & Carroll, J. S. (2007). Collaborating for systemic change. *MIT Sloan Management Review, 48*(2), 44–53. Retrieved from www.sloanreview.mit.edu/article/collaborating-for-systemic-change/

Sergiovanni, T. J. (1992). Why we should seek substitutes for leadership. *Educational Leadership, 49*(5), 41–45.

Sergiovanni, T. J. (2005). *Strengthening the heartbeat: Leading and learning together in schools.* Jossey-Bass.

Sergiovanni, T. J., & Carver, F. D. (1973). *The new school executive: A theory of administration.* Dodd, Mead & Co.

Shaked, H., & Schechter, C. (2016). Systems thinking among school middle leaders. *Educational Management Administration & Leadership, 45*(4), 699–718.

Shantz, D., & Pruieur, P. D. (1996). Teacher professionalism and school leadership: An antithesis? *Education (Chula Vista, Calif.), 116*(3), 393–396.

Shatzer, R. H., Caldarella, P., Hallam, P. R., & Brown, B. L. (2013). Comparing the effects of instructional and transformational leadership on student achievement: Implications for practice. *Educational Management Administration & Leadership, 42*(4), 445–459. https://doi.org/10.1177/1741143213502192

Shen, J. (1999). Connecting educational theory, research, and practice: A comprehensive review of John I. Goodlad's publications. *Journal of Thought, 34*(4), 25–96.

Shen, J. (2001). Teacher and principal empowerment: National, longitudinal, and comparative perspectives. *Educational Horizons, 79*(3), 124–129. Reprinted with permission as Shen, J. (2005). Principals' and teachers' power. In J. Shen, et al. (Eds.), *School principals* (pp. 106–116). Peter Lang.

Shen, J. (2015). Summaries and reflections: Toward school renewal. In J. Shen & W. L. Burt (Eds.), *Learning-centered school leadership: School renewal in action* (pp. 209–222). Peter Lang.

Shen, J. (2020). The theory of bifurcated educational system and its implications for school improvement. *International Journal of Leadership in Education.* https://doi.org/10.1080/13603124.2020.1808708

Shen, J., & Burt, W. (Eds.). (2015). *Learning-centered leadership: School renewal in action.* Peter Lang.

Shen, J., & Cooley, V. E. (2008). Critical issues in using data for decision-making. *International Journal of Leadership in Education, 11*(3), 319–329.

Shen, J., & Cooley, V. E. (Eds.). (2013). *A resource book for improving principals' learning-centered leadership.* Peter Lang.

Shen, J., & Cooley, V. E. (2015). Facilitating school renewal via the Learning-centered leadership development program: An introduction. In J. Shen & W. Burt (Eds.), *Learning-centered school leadership: School renewal in action* (pp. 3–21). Peter Lang.

Shen, J., & Cooley, V. E. (Eds.). (2012). *A resource book for learning-centered leadership*. New York, NY: Peter Lang.

Shen, J., & Cooley, V. E. (2012). Learning-centered leadership development program for practicing and aspiring principals. In K. L. Sanzo, S. Myran, & A. H. Nomoore (Eds.), *Successful school leadership preparation and development: Lessons learned from US DoE school leadership program grants* (pp. 113–135). Emerald Group.

Shen, J., & Ma, X. (2006). Does systemic change work? Curricular and instructional practice in the context of systemic change. *School Leadership and Policy, 5*(3), 231–256.

Shen, J., & Wu, H. (2024). The relationship between principal leadership and student achievement: A multivariate meta-analysis with an emphasis on conceptual models and methodological approaches. *Educational Administration Quarterly.* https://doi.org/10.1177/0013161X241286527

Shen, J., & Xia, J. (2012). The relationship between teachers' and principals' power: Is it a win-win situation or zero-sum game? *International Journal of Leadership in Education 15*(2), 153–174.

Shen, J., Cooley, V., Ma, X., Reeves, P., Burt, W., Rainey, J. M., & Yuan, W. (2012). Data-informed decision-making on high-impact strategies: Developing and validating an instrument for Principals. *Journal of Experimental Education, 80*(1), 1–25.

Shen, J., Cooley, V., Reeves, P., Burt, W., Ryan, L., Rainey, J. M., & Yuan, W. (2010). Using data for decision-making: Perspectives from 16 principals in Michigan, USA. *International Review of Education, 56*, 435–456.

Shen, J., Gao, X., & Xia, J. (2017). School as a loosely coupled organization? An empirical examination using national SASS 2003–04 data. *Educational Management, Administration & Leadership, 45*(4), 657–681.

Shen, J., Kavanaugh, A. L., Wegenke, G. L., Rodriguez-Campos, L., Rincones-Gomez, R., Palmer, L. B., Crawford, C., Cooley, V. E., Poppink, S., VanderJagt, D., Hsieh, C., Ruhl-Smith, C. D., Keiser, N. M., & Portin, B. S. (2005). *School principals.* New York, NY: Peter Lang.

Shen, J., Ma, X., Cooley, V. E., & Burt, W. L. (2016a). Measuring principals' data-informed decision-making on high-impact strategies: Validating an instrument used by teachers. *Journal of School Leadership, 26*(3), 407–436.

Shen, J., Ma, X., Cooley, V. E., & Burt, W. L. (2016b). Mediating effects of school process on the relationship between principals' data-informed decision-making and student achievement. *International Journal of Leadership in Education, 19*(4), 373–401.

Shen, J., Ma, X., Gao, X., Palmer, B., Poppink, S., Burt, W., Leneway, R., McCrumb, D., Pearson, C., Rainey, M., Reeves, P., & Wegenke, G. (2018). Developing and validating an instrument measuring school leadership. *Educational Studies, 45*(4), 401–421. https://doi.org/10.1080/03055698.2018.1446338

Shen, J., Ma, X., Mansberger, N., Bierlein Palmer, L., Burt, W., Leneway, R., Reeves, P., Poppink, S., McCrumb, D., Whitten, E., Gao, X., & Wu, H. (2024). Developing and validating an instrument measuring school renewal: Testing the factorial validity and reliability. *International Journal of Leadership in Education, 27*(4), 875–893. https://doi.org/10.1080/13603124.2021.1930187

Shen, J., Ma, X., Mansberger, N., Gao, X., Palmer, L. B., Burt, W., … Whitten, E. (2020). Testing the predictive power of an instrument titled "Orientation to School Renewal." *School Effectiveness and School Improvement, 31*(4), 505–528. https://doi.org/10.1080/09243453.2020.1749087

Shen, J., Palmer, L., & Crawford, C. (2005). The importance of educational goals as perceived by principals. In J. Shen (Ed.), *School principals* (pp. 46–60). Peter Lang.

Shen, J., Wu, H., Reeves, P., Zheng, Y., Ryan, L., & Anderson, D. (2020). The association between teacher leadership and student achievement: A meta-analysis. *Educational Research Review, 31*(2020), 100357. https://doi.org/10.1016/j.edurev.2020.100357

Shen, J., Yang, H., Cao, H., & Warfield, C. (2008). The fidelity-adaptation relationship in non-evidence-based programs and its implication for program evaluation. *Evaluation, 14*(4), 467–481.

Shin, J., Espin, C. A., Deno, S. L., & McConnell, S. (2004). Use of hierarchical linear modeling and curriculum-based measurement for assessing academic growth and instructional factors for students with learning difficulties. *Asia Pacific Education Review, 5*(2), 136–148.

Shores, K., & Steinberg, M. P. (2022). Fiscal federalism and K–12 education funding: Policy lessons from two educational crises. *Educational Researcher, 51*(8), 551–558.

Silva, D. Y., Gimbert, B., & Nolan, J. (2002). Sliding the doors: Locking and unlocking possibilities for teacher leadership. *Teachers College Record, 102*(4), 779–804.

Sirotnik, K. (1999). Making sense of educational renewal. *The Phi Delta Kappan, 80*(8), 606–610.

Slavin, R. E., Cheung, A., Holmes, G., Madden, N. A., & Chamberlain, A. (2013). Effects of a data-driven district reform model on state assessment outcomes. *American Educational Research Journal, 50*(2), 371–396. https://doi.org/10.3102/0002831212466909.

Sleegers, P., & Wesselingh, A. (1995). Dutch dilemmas: Decentralisation, school autonomy and professionalisation of teachers. *Educational Review, 47*(2), 199–207. https://doi.org/10.1080/0013191950470207

Smith, M. S., & O'Day, J. A. (1990). Systemic school reform. In S. Fuhrman & B. Malen (Eds.), *The politics of curriculum and testing* (pp. 233–267). The Falmer Press.

Smith, T., Cobb, P., Farran, D., Cordray, D., & Munter, C. (2013). Evaluating math recovery: Assessing the causal impact of a diagnostic tutoring program on student achievement. *American Educational Research Journal, 50*, 397–428.

Smith, W., Guarino, A., Strom, P., & Adams, O. (2006). Effective teaching and learning environments and principal self-efficacy. *Journal of Research for Educational Leaders, 3*(2), 4–23.

Soder, R. (1999). When words find their meaning: Renewal versus reform. *The Phi Delta Kappan, 80*(8), 568–570.

Southworth, G. (2002). Instructional leadership in schools: Reflections and empirical evidence. *School Leadership and Management, 22*(1), 73–91.

Spillane, J. P. (1994). How districts mediate between state policy and teachers' practice. In R. F. Elmore & S. H. Fuhrman (Eds.), *The governance of curriculum: 1994 yearbook of the Association for Supervision and Curriculum Development* (pp. 167–185). Alexandria, VA: Association for Supervision and Curriculum Development.

Spillane, J. P. (1998). State policy and the non-monolithic nature of the local school district: Organizational and professional considerations. *American Educational Research Journal, 35*(1), 33–63. https://doi.org/10.3102/00028312035001033

Spillane, J. P. (1999). External reform initiatives and teachers' efforts to reconstruct their practice: The mediating role of teachers' zones of enactment. *Journal of Curriculum Studies, 31*(2), 143–175.

Spillane, J. P. (2006). *Distributed leadership.* Jossey-Bass.

Spillane, J. P. (2012). Data in practice: Conceptualizing the data-based decision-making phenomena. *American Journal of Education, 118*(2), 113–141.

Spillane, J. P., & Coldren, A. F. (2015). *Diagnosis and design for school improvement: Using a distributed perspective to lead and manage change.* Teachers College Press.

Spillane, J. P., Halverson, R., & Diamond, J. B. (2001). Investigating school leadership practice: A distributed perspective. *Educational Researcher, 30*(3), 23–28.

Spillane, J. P., Parise, L. M., & Sherer, J. Z. (2011). Organizational routines as coupling mechanisms: Policy, school administration, and the technical core. *American Educational Research Journal, 48*(3), 586–619.

Starratt, R. J. (1996). *Transforming educational administration: Meaning, community and excellence.* New York, NY: McGraw-Hill.

Stodolsky, S. S., & Grossman, P. L. (1995). The impact of subject matter on curricular activity: An analysis of five academic subjects. *American Educational Research Journal, 32*(2), 227–250.

Stoll, L., Bolam, R., McMahon, A., Wallace, M., & Thomas, S. (2006). Professional learning communities: A review of the literature. *Journal of Educational Change, 7*(4), 221–258.

Stone, M., Horejs, J., & Lomas, A. (1997). Commonalities and differences in teacher leadership at the elementary, middle, and high school levels. *Action in Teacher Education, 19*(3), 49–64.

Strahan, D. (2003). Promoting a collaborative professional culture in three elementary schools that have beaten the odds. *The Elementary School Journal, 104*(2), 127–146.

Strain, P. S., & Bovey, E. H., II. (2011). Randomized, controlled trial of the LEAP model of early intervention for young children with autism spectrum disorders. *Topics in Early Childhood Special Education, 31*(3), 133–154. https://doi.org/10.1177/0271121411408740

Stringfield, S., Reynolds, D., & Schaffer, E. (2008). Improving secondary students' academic achievement through a focus on reform reliability: 4- and 9-year findings from the High Reliability Schools project. *School Effectiveness and School Improvement, 19*(4), 409–428.

Sunderman, G. L., & Kim, J. S. (2007). The expansion of federal power and the politics of implementing the No Child Left Behind Act. *Teachers College Record, 109*(5), 1057–1085.

Supovitz, J. A., & Klein, V. (2003). *Mapping a course for improved student learning: How innovative schools systematically use student performance data to guide improvement.* Philadelphia, PA: Consortium for Policy Research in Education.

Supovitz, J., Sirinides, P., & May, H. (2010). How principals and peers influence teaching and learning. *Educational Administration Quarterly, 46*(1), 31–56.

Sweetland, S. R., & Hoy, W. K. (2000). School characteristics and educational outcomes: Toward an organizational model of student achievement in middle schools. *Educational Administration Quarterly, 36*(5), 703–729. https://doi.org/10.1177/00131610021969173

Swindler, N. H. (2009). Middle school cultures and student achievement. (Publication No. 3383762) (Doctoral dissertation, The University of Southern Mississippi). ProQuest Dissertations & Theses Global.

Tan, C. Y. (2016). Examining school leadership effects on student achievement: The role of contextual challenges and constraints. *Cambridge Journal of Education, 25*(3), 451–468.

Tan, C. Y., Dimmock, C., & Walker, A. (2024). How school leadership practices relate to student outcomes: Insights from a three-level meta-analysis. *Educational Management Administration & Leadership, 52*(1), 6–27.

Tan, C. Y., Gao, L., & Shi, M. (2020). Second-order meta-analysis synthesizing the evidence on associations between school leadership and different school outcomes. *Educational Management Administration and Leadership.* https://doi.org/10.1177/1741143220935456

Tannenbaum, R., & Schmidt, W. (1958). How to choose a leadership pattern. *Harvard Business Review, 36*(2), 95–101.

Thorn, C. A. (2001). Knowledge management for educational information systems. *Education Policy Analysis Archives, 9,* 47.

Thornton, B., & Perreault, G. (2002). Becoming a data-based leader: An introduction. *NASSP Bulletin, 86*(630), 86–96.

US Department of Education. (2011). *Fast facts.* Retrieved July 3, 2011, from www.nces.ed.gov/fastfacts/display.asp?id=28

U.S. Department of Education. (2012). *Investing in America's future: A blueprint for transforming career and technical education.*

U.S. Department of Education. (n.d.). *Using data to influence classroom decisions.* Retrieved July 1, 2012, from www2.ed.gov/teachers/nclbguide/datadriven.pdf

Van Geel, M., Keuning, T., Visscher, A. J., & Fox, J.-P. (2016). Assessing the effects of a school-wide data-based decision-making intervention on student achievement growth in primary schools. *American Educational Research Journal, 53*(2), 360–394. https://doi.org/10.3102/0002831216637346

Wahlstrom, K. L., & Louis, K. S. (2008). How teachers experience principal leadership: The roles of professional community, trust, efficacy, and shared responsibility. *Educational Administration Quarterly, 44*(4), 458–495.

Wang, M., & Long, Q. (2011). Modified robust variance estimator for generalized estimating equations with improved small-sample performance. *Statistics in Medicine, 30*(11), 1278–1291.

Weick, K. E. (1976). Educational organizations as loosely coupled systems. *Administrative Science Quarterly, 21,* 1–19.

Weick, K. E. (1984). Management of organizational change among loosely controlled elements. In P. Goodman (Ed.), *Change in organizations* (pp. 375–409). Jossey-Bass.

Wenner, J. A., & Campbell, T. (2017). The theoretical and empirical basis of teacher leadership: A review of the literature. *Review of Educational Research, 87*(1), 134–171.

Whitt, K., Scheurich, J. J., & Skrla, L. (2015). Understanding superintendents' self-efficacy influences on instructional leadership and student achievement. *Journal of School Leadership, 25,* 102–131.

Witziers, B., Bosker, R. J., & Krüger, M. L. (2003). Educational leadership and student achievement: The elusive search for an association. *Educational Administration Quarterly, 39*(3), 398–425.

Wohlstetter, P., Malloy, C., Chau, D., & Polhemus, J. (2003). Improving schools through networks: A new approach to urban school reform. *Educational Policy, 17*(4), 399–430.

Woodland, R., Lee, M. K., & Randall, J. (2013). A validation study of the teacher collaboration assessment survey. *Educational Research and Evaluation, 19*(5), 442–460.

Wu, H., Gao, X., & Shen, J. (2019). Principal leadership effects on student achievement: A multilevel analysis using Programme for International Student Assessment 2015 data. *Educational Studies, 45*(4), 402–421.

Wu, H., & Shen, J. (2022). The association between principal leadership and student achievement: A multivariate meta-meta-analysis. *Educational Research Review, 35*(4). https://doi.org/10.1016/j.edurev.2021.100423

Wu, H., Shen, J., Zhang, Y., & Zheng, Y. (2020). Examining the effect of principal leadership on student science achievement. *International Journal of Science Education, 42*(6), 1017–1039.

Xia, J., & Shen, J. (2020). The principal-teacher's power relationship revisited: A national study based on the 2011–12 SASS data. *Leadership and Policy in Schools, 19*(3), 477–496. https://doi.org/10.1080/15700763.2019.1586962

York-Barr, J., & Duke, K. (2004). What do we know about teacher leadership? Findings from two decades of scholarship. *Review of Educational Research, 74*(3), 255–316.

Yukl, G. A. (1989). *Leadership in organizations* (2nd ed.). Upper Saddle River, NJ: Prentice Hall.

Zeinabadi, H. R. (2014). Principal-teacher high-quality exchange indicators and student achievement: Testing a model. *Journal of Educational Administration, 52*(3), 404–420.

Zepeda, S. J., Mayers, R. S., & Benson, B. N. (2013). *The call to teacher leadership*. Routledge.

Zheng, Y., Shen, J., & Li, X. (2024). The relationship between teacher-to-teacher relationship and student achievement: A meta-analysis. *Research Papers in Education.* https://doi.org/10.1080/02671522.2024.2349990

Index

www.ingramcontent.com/pod-product-compliance
Ingram Content Group UK Ltd.
Pitfield, Milton Keynes, MK11 3LW, UK
UKHW022137210626
472488UK00010B/143